THE *Smirnoff* BRUNCH BOOK

A Benjamin Company/Rutledge Book

Fred R. Sammis	Publisher
John T. Sammis	Associate Publisher
Hyla O'Connor	Consultant
Doris M. Townsend	Editor-in-Chief
Allan Mogel	Art Director
Marilyn Weber	Managing Editor
Arthur Gubernick	Production Manager
Jeanne McClow	Copy Editor
Diane Matheson	Production Associate
Myra Poznick	Art Associate

All photographs by Walter Storck Studios, Inc.

Easter Eggs, page 45, by Joann Foster

Fondue Pots, page 81, by Catherineholm

Drawings by Harry Rosenbaum

On the Cover: Bloody Mary, Greek Fassolia me Arni, eggs, Hot Cross Buns, cooked lobster, French goat cheese

CONTENTS

THE *Smirnoff*
BRUNCH BOOK

COME, FRIENDS, BRUNCH IS SERVED!

by S. I. Hayakawa

The idea of brunch, as it is developed so thoroughly in this entertaining work, throws much light on the richness of our multicultural heritage. As a nation of immigrants, we have many different traditions in food, in drinks, in condiments and sauces, in manners of serving. What makes us all Americans is the way in which we have all borrowed so freely from each other. As a nonprofessional but committed practitioner of the art of cooking—and eating what I cook—I find special joy in comparing my knowledge with the culinary lore of others.

Many persons nowadays are on a four-day workweek, and therefore enjoy a three-day weekend. Many more will be on this schedule as time passes. Some will take advantage of their increased leisure with early morning golf dates and fishing expeditions. But surely many will also find more frequent occasions for brunch.

For brunch is a very civilized happening. Unlike the cocktail hour, when it is both appropriate and sometimes even necessary to deaden the anxieties and frustrations of the day with quick-acting and powerful potations, brunch is an occasion to enjoy well rested and with peace of mind. It suggests, therefore, the lighter and less devastating things to drink, designed not to overwhelm or anesthetize, but to stimulate.

Brunch may prove eventually to be a corrective to the all-too-conventional, standardized American breakfast. Not that there is anything wrong with eggs with ham, bacon or sausages, but there is something terribly wrong with having no alternatives. I recall a resort hotel on the island of Maui in Hawaii. The seas thereabouts were full of fantastic fish—kumu and kawakawa and moi and ulna—and the island was full of Japanese capable of doing interesting things with them. But the breakfast menu at the hotel offered only eggs with ham, bacon or sausage.

I recall, too, my stay at a hotel in Miami Beach. The previous afternoon I had caught several king mackerel a mile or two offshore. I cleaned them and gave them to the chef to prepare for me for breakfast. The platter of golden fried fish was far more than my friend and I could eat, so I asked our waitress if she would pass the platter around to others in the dining room. "Nothing doing," she said. "We'll eat the rest—Irma and Elaine and I." And the girls did. They, too, welcomed a change from the eggs with ham, bacon or sausage on the menu. Perhaps the example of brunch will some day break down the deadly uniformity of American breakfasts.

The possibilities are enormous. From the British we have kippered herring and broiled kidneys. From the Scotch finnan haddie. I don't know who originated smoked cod but when steamed and served with butter and boiled potatoes, there are few things more satisfactory. Deep in western American tradition are hangtown fry (eggs, oysters, bacon), steak and eggs and quick-fried beef liver, served hot on slices of white bread.

From Jewish cuisine we get blintzes—cheese blintzes, meat blintzes, served with sour cream. Also lox (smoked salmon) with cream cheese and bagels. Sausages from Poland and Germany, Welsh rarebit, quiche Lorraine, cold poached salmon, can all be faced at brunch if preceded by a Ramos fizz, a sangria or a screwdriver and if not served before 10:30 A.M. Danish smørrebrød (open-faced sandwiches) and a cheese board—with rye or black bread—also produce a fine philosophical frame of mind with which to face the day.

From Mexico we have *huevos rancheros* (ranch-style eggs), which is gently fried eggs on a tortilla, covered with *salsa*, a hot sauce that comes in varying degrees of potency. I always think, when I start the morning with *huevos rancheros*, that I am not going to be able to face it—but I always end up with seconds.

The great Chinese contribution to the art of late morning nourishment is, of course, the *dim sum* luncheon, served at any time from about eleven in the morning into the early afternoon in the Chinatowns of San Francisco, Chicago, New York, Los Angeles and elsewhere. *Dim sum* are ravioli-like envelopes of translucent pasta filled with chopped, flavored meats and seafood and vegetables, wonderfully varied in ingredients and shape and flavor. Every *dim sum* luncheon is an adventure because each restaurant has, in addition to traditional and expected delicacies, its own specialties.

If you want to go Japanese in your brunch, try salt-broiled fish—salmon steak, rock cod or small whole trout—with *misoshiru* (Japanese bean soup), pickles and rice.

I endorse the brunch as delineated in this book as an institution with a promising future. Brunch is for the young—and the young in heart. Brunch is for the innovative—and for those who would grace their lives with ceremony. Breakfast clubs, service club lunches, formal dinners, all have their uses in a busy and complex society. Brunches, perhaps more than any other meal, are for their own sake.

YOU—THE BRUNCH EXPERT

WELCOME—OR GOOD-BYE

You—the brunch expert—always know the perfect way to say "Welcome" or "Bon Voyage" or "We're sorry that you're moving." This time you're having a brunch for the brand new family in the house next door to say "Welcome to the neighborhood and we hope you will be happy here." This is an adaptable brunch—delightful in summer or in winter, suited to serving outdoors as well as indoors. It is planned here for eight people, but if you want to invite more of the neighbors, it can easily be adapted to include a large crowd.

Smirnoff Bloody Marys
Mushroom-Tarragon Eggs   Cider-baked Canadian Bacon
Toasted French Bread
Quick Crescents   Papaya with Lemon Wedges
Coffee

SMIRNOFF BLOODY MARY   1 drink

1½ ounces Smirnoff Vodka	**Pinch each salt, pepper,**
3 ounces tomato juice	**celery salt**
Juice of ½ lemon	½ teaspoon A.1. Sauce

Combine all ingredients and shake well with cracked ice. Strain into a 6-ounce old-fashioned glass over ice cubes.

MUSHROOM-TARRAGON EGGS   8 servings

2 pounds mushrooms	1 teaspoon dried tarragon
½ cup butter	1½ cups heavy cream
2 tablespoons minced onion	16 Eggs Mollet (page 138), shelled
2 tablespoons tarragon vinegar	

Wash mushrooms and pat dry. Trim stems and cut into slices through both stems and caps. Melt butter in a large skillet and sauté mushroom slices lightly. Remove mushrooms and reserve. To the skillet add the onion, vinegar and tarragon and boil rapidly until dry. Add cream and cook over high heat, stirring constantly, until reduced to about 1 cup. Reserve. Arrange the mushrooms in slices around the edges of 8 individual

baking dishes. Place 2 eggs into center of each mushroom ring. Spoon about a tablespoon of the reserved sauce over each egg. Bake in a preheated 350° oven for 8 minutes, or until heated. Serve immediately.
Helpful to know: Save the mushroom trimmings for some other use— cream of mushroom soup, perhaps.

CIDER-BAKED CANADIAN BACON
12 to 14 servings

¾ cup light brown sugar
1 teaspoon dry mustard
2 tablespoons fine, dry bread crumbs
1 tablespoon cider vinegar

1 piece Canadian bacon, about 3 pounds
¾ cup apple cider

Combine sugar, mustard, bread crumbs and vinegar, and reserve. Bake bacon uncovered in a preheated 350° oven for 1½ hours, basting every 15 minutes with the cider. Spread brown-sugar mixture over bacon and bake for about 20 minutes, or until the mixture has glazed the bacon. Serve hot.
Helpful to know: Canned Danish Canadian bacon is delicious. It will not take as much time to cook—just heat through, then spread with sugar mixture to glaze.

QUICK CRESCENTS
16 crescents

2 packages (8 ounces each) refrigerated crescent dinner rolls
1 cup almond paste

1 egg, slightly beaten
1 cup sliced, blanched almonds

Separate dough into 16 triangles. On a lightly floured surface, roll out almond paste to a 6- x 20-inch rectangle (or roll out half at a time if you prefer and space is limited). Cut into eight 6- x 2½-inch rectangles, then cut each rectangle in half diagonally to make 16 triangles. Lay 1 almond-paste triangle on each triangle of dough. Starting at narrowest side, roll up to a point. Place on lightly oiled cookie sheet with point underneath. Brush with egg; sprinkle with almonds. Bake in a preheated 375° oven for 10 to 12 minutes, or until golden.

STRICTLY FOR SHOW-OFFS

You have these people you want to impress, right? First, invite them for brunch rather than for dinner or to an evening party—brunch is the "in" way to entertain. Then exert yourself a little, although the food you're going to offer these new friends only *looks* (and tastes) as if you'd spent hours of labor over a hot stove. Set a special table: If you have—or can borrow—an obi, the handsome sash with which the Japanese hold their kimonos in place, use it as a runner for the table and complement it with mats and napkins in a color that lives well with it. Pile shiny lemons and limes in a low bowl and stick single lemon leaves and single blue bachelor's buttons in the spaces between the fruit.

Smirnoff Martinis on the Rocks
Hospitality Wafers   Stuffed and Ripe Olives
Artichokes with Lamb Stuffing   Avgolemono Sauce
Tomato Aspic with Homemade Russian Dressing
Mango Chutney   Rye Toast with Sweet Butter
Orange Baba   Coffee

SMIRNOFF MARTINI ON THE ROCKS

1 drink

2 ounces Smirnoff Vodka   Twist of lemon
¼ ounce dry vermouth

Combine vodka and vermouth. Pour over ice cubes in an old-fashioned glass. Garnish with twist of lemon.

HOSPITALITY WAFERS

3 dozens

¾ cup butter, softened   ½ clove garlic, minced
½ cup shredded Cheddar cheese   1 teaspoon snipped parsley
⅓ cup crumbled bleu cheese   1 teaspoon snipped chives
2 cups sifted flour

Cream together butter and both cheeses. Mix in flour, garlic, parsley and chives. With the hands, shape into rolls 1½ inches in diameter. Wrap in aluminum foil or plastic wrap and chill. Slice in ¼-inch slices and bake in preheated 375° oven for 8 to 10 minutes.

ARTICHOKES WITH LAMB STUFFING

4 servings

4 whole fresh artichokes   ¼ cup snipped parsley
2 tablespoons white vinegar   2 eggs, beaten
1 pound ground lamb   ¼ teaspoon cinnamon
¾ cup chopped onion   ½ teaspoon salt
2 tablespoons cooking oil   Avgolemono Sauce
½ cup fine, dry bread crumbs

Wash artichokes. Cut off stems evenly, close to the base. Cook in boiling salted water, with white vinegar, 25 to 30 minutes, or until a leaf can be readily pulled off. Drain upside down on paper towels. Using kitchen scissors, cut off spiny top part of each leaf. Using a teaspoon, remove small center leaves and choke—the thistlelike part at the inner base of the artichoke. Brown lamb and onion in hot oil. Drain. Add crumbs, parsley, eggs, cinnamon and salt. Mix well. Spread artichoke leaves slightly and stuff with lamb mixture. Place in 9- x 9- x 2-inch pan and pour in 1 inch of hot water. Bake in preheated 375° oven for 25 to 30 minutes. Serve with Avgolemono Sauce.
Helpful to know: You can prepare and stuff the artichokes in advance; bake just before serving; extend baking time 10 minutes.

11

AVGOLEMONO SAUCE
4 servings

2 cups chicken bouillon
3 eggs

3 tablespoons lemon juice

Pour bouillon into saucepan. In a bowl, beat eggs with lemon juice. Heat bouillon and add ½ cup of it slowly to eggs, beating constantly. Return eggs to remaining bouillon, stirring constantly. Heat, but do not boil. Serve at once.

TOMATO ASPIC
4 servings

1 envelope unflavored gelatin
2 cups tomato juice
¼ cup chopped onion
2 tablespoons snipped celery leaves
1 tablespoon light brown sugar
½ teaspoon salt

1 small bay leaf
2 whole cloves
1½ tablespoons lemon juice
½ cup finely chopped celery
Homemade Russian Dressing
(page 88)

Soften gelatin in ½ cup tomato juice. Mix 1½ cups tomato juice with onion, celery leaves, sugar, salt, bay leaf and cloves. Heat just to boiling; strain. Add gelatin and stir until dissolved. Stir in lemon juice. Chill until partially set. Add celery. Pour into a 3-cup mold. Chill until firm. Serve with Homemade Russian Dressing.

ORANGE BABA
6 to 8 servings

1 package (13¾ ounces) hot-roll mix
⅓ cup sugar
6 tablespoons butter, softened
2 eggs

1 can (6 ounces) frozen orange juice concentrate, undiluted
1 cup sugar

Prepare hot-roll mix according to package directions. Stir in ⅓ cup sugar and the butter. Beat in eggs thoroughly, 1 at a time. Place in well-oiled 6½-cup gugelhupf mold. Cover and let rise in a warm place, free from draft, until almost doubled in bulk, 30 to 45 minutes. Bake in preheated 400° oven for 30 minutes. (If necessary, cover with aluminum foil the last 10 minutes of cooking to keep from browning too much.) In a saucepan combine orange juice, 1 cup sugar and 1 cup water. Bring to a full boil. Remove from heat. Turn baba out of mold onto a shallow pan. Immediately spoon orange-juice mixture over it. Keep basting with syrup until the baba has absorbed all of it. Garnish with almonds if desired. Cool.

VACATION SPECIAL

The children are all off to camp, and it's time to do something just for yourself. So, invite three other couples for brunch, close friends of yours, because you're going to ask your guests to cook. The women, that is. What are the men going to do? Make the drinks. Serve the drinks. Talk until called to the table. Some of the food you can prepare in advance, of course. Make the cake at least the day before. Have the melons halved, seeded and chilling (in plastic bags, so that they don't distribute their fragrance where it's not wanted) in the refrigerator. Hard-cook the eggs the day before (page 137) and have them shelled and waiting. Divide the chores this way: One of you will prepare the Pancake Puffs, one the Rancho Sauce, one the Scotch Eggs, and the fourth can attend to the melon balls and also grate the cheese. (Don't forget—one of you put the coffee on!) What will you do while you prepare the meal? Talk—what else?

Smirnoff Cape Codders
Minted Cantaloupe Balls
Scotch Eggs with French-fried Parsley
Pancake Puffs with Rancho Sauce
Mocha Wonder Cake (page 58)   Coffee

SMIRNOFF CAPE CODDER
1 drink

1½ ounces Smirnoff Vodka
3 ounces cranberry juice

Juice of ½ lime
Carbonated water

Combine vodka with cranberry and lime juices over ice cubes in an 8-ounce glass. Fill with carbonated water.

MINTED CANTALOUPE BALLS
8 servings

3 medium-size cantaloupes

16 sprigs mint

Cut cantaloupes into balls with a melon-ball cutter or the bowl of a small spoon. Divide among 8 serving dishes. Chop half of mint and sprinkle over melon balls. Garnish each dish with sprig of mint.

SCOTCH EGGS
8 servings

8 medium-size eggs,
    hard-cooked (page 137)
1½ pounds sausage meat

1 egg, slightly beaten
¾ cup fine, dry bread crumbs
    Oil or shortening for deep-fat frying

Shell eggs. Using your hands, flatten sausage meat on a floured board and cut into 8 pieces. Mold 1 piece of sausage meat around each egg, rolling and stretching meat in your hands until egg is completely covered. Dip sausage-covered eggs in beaten egg, then into bread crumbs. Deep-fry in oil heated to 370° about 4 or 5 minutes, or until sausage is deep brown.

FRENCH-FRIED PARSLEY
8 servings

1 bunch parsley
    Oil or shortening for deep-fat frying

Salt

Wash parsley and dry well—paper towels are fine for this. Break apart into individual sprigs, and fry the sprigs in fat heated to 370° for only about 3 seconds. Drain on more paper towels and salt well. Serve with Scotch Eggs.

PANCAKE PUFFS
8 servings

6 eggs
6 tablespoons flour
1 tablespoon sugar

¾ cup milk
½ cup butter
Juice of 1 lemon

Beat eggs, flour, sugar and milk with rotary or electric beater until well blended. Divide butter into each of 2 large, shallow baking dishes and melt. Pour half of batter into each dish. Bake in preheated 425° oven for 8 minutes. Reduce heat to 375° and bake about 8 minutes more, or until pancakes are puffed over sides of pan and lightly browned. Remove to hot serving platter, sprinkle with lemon juice and roll up lightly. To serve, cut each pancake into 4 sections.

RANCHO SAUCE
8 servings

1 can (2 pounds, 3 ounces) plum
   tomatoes
½ can (6-ounce size) tomato paste
2 tablespoons finely grated onion
½ teaspoon crumbled basil

½ teaspoon sugar
1 cup coarsely chopped mushrooms
   Salt to taste
¾ cup grated Monterey Jack cheese

Strain tomatoes and discard juice. Add remaining ingredients except mushrooms and cheese and bring to a boil. Simmer 10 minutes. Add mushrooms, taste for seasoning and simmer gently 10 minutes longer. Serve sauce over Pancake Puff servings, sprinkling each serving with cheese.

SPOIL THE FAMILY

Surprise the family with a special brunch just for them. The stars of the meal are tempting sweet rolls, relatives of Danish pastry, that are easy to make and can be whipped together in advance. The eggs take little time to prepare and need no watching as they cook, so that you can safely keep an eye on the grilling ham. The mushrooms can be sautéed in advance and finished at the last minute. All in all, although it's really an easy meal to put together, it's the kind that looks and tastes as though you'd spent dedicated days slaving over it just to spoil the family.

Smirnoff Screwdrivers
Hidden Eggs   Grilled Ham Slices
California Mushrooms
Tossed Green Salad
Marmalade Snails   Cinnamon-Raisin Snails
Coffee

SMIRNOFF SCREWDRIVER

1 drink

2 ounces Smirnoff Vodka   **Orange juice**

Place 2 or 3 cubes of ice in a 6-ounce glass. Add vodka. Fill glass with orange juice. Stir.

HIDDEN EGGS

8 servings

8 small, firm-ripe tomatoes
¼ cup snipped parsley
¼ cup butter

1 large onion, chopped
8 eggs
Salt and pepper to taste

Cut tops from tomatoes. Scoop out pulp and turn shells upside down to drain. Discard seeds, chop pulp and mix with parsley. Melt butter in a skillet and sauté onion in it until soft but not browned; add tomato pulp and season to taste. Stir well and divide mixture into the tomato shells. Gently break 1 egg into each tomato shell and season lightly. Place in a 9- x 12½- x 2-inch pan which has been lightly oiled. Add ¼ cup water. Bake in a preheated 375° oven until eggs are set to your liking.

CALIFORNIA MUSHROOMS

8 servings

1½ pounds mushrooms
¼ cup butter
Salt and white pepper to taste

1 cup dairy sour cream
2 tablespoons chopped fresh dill *or* 2 teaspoons dried dillweed

Wash mushrooms and pat dry. Trim stems if necessary and cut into slices through both cap and stem. Melt butter in a large skillet and sauté mushrooms in it until lightly browned. (At this point you may leave them—the heat turned off, of course—until just before serving time. Heat, and continue.) Turn heat low; season mushrooms lightly with salt and pepper. Distribute sour cream over mushrooms in spoonfuls and stir in. Heat, but do not allow to boil. Garnish with dillweed. Serve at once.

SNAILS

2 dozens

**2 packages (8 ounces each) refrigerated buttermilk biscuits
Orange marmalade
Chopped walnuts**

**2 eggs, beaten
Butter, softened
Sugar
Cinnamon
½ cup white raisins**

17

Arrange biscuits from 1 package in 2 rows of 5 biscuits each on a lightly floured surface. Roll out to a 12- x 6-inch rectangle. Spread with orange marmalade; sprinkle with walnuts. Roll up, as you would a jelly roll, starting on one long side; moisten edge and press gently to seal the roll. Cut into twelve 1-inch slices. Place, cut side down, on lightly oiled baking sheet, and brush with egg. Repeat with second package of biscuits, spreading with butter and sprinkling with sugar, cinnamon and raisins. Bake in a preheated 375° oven for 12 to 15 minutes, or until golden.

A BLISS OF BLINTZES

Bridge is planned for the early afternoon, and the card players need a good meal to give them energy for the fray. Don't invite anyone who isn't a bridge nut or, if you do, have Scrabble ready to entertain those who are put off by the very thought of bridge. The meal is easy: The blintzes can be made and filled ahead of time and finished "to order," while the bacon grills, when the guests are ready to eat. Making the breakfast cake, a truly superb coffee bread, is a day-before task. The tomatoes will be all the better for a couple of hours mellowing in the refrigerator. Set the table early, and you'll be wondering how to occupy yourself till the guests come!

Smirnoff Smashes

Cheese-filled Blintzes	*Sour Cream*
Strawberry Preserve	*Applesauce*
Grilled Canadian Bacon	*Basil Tomatoes*
Breakfast Cake	*Coffee*

SMIRNOFF SMASH

1 drink

1 lump sugar
1 ounce carbonated water
4 sprigs mint

2 ounces Smirnoff Vodka
Twist of lemon peel

Muddle sugar lump with carbonated water and mint in a 6-ounce old-fashioned glass. Add vodka and ice. Stir. Decorate with lemon twist.

CHEESE-FILLED BLINTZES

8 large blintzes

3 eggs
1 cup milk
½ teaspoon salt
2 tablespoons salad oil

¾ cup flour
Butter
Cheese Filling

Beat eggs, milk, salt and salad oil together. Stir the flour into egg mixture until well blended. Heat about 1 teaspoon butter in a 10-inch omelet pan or skillet; pour in about ¼ cup of the batter, quickly tilting pan to spread the batter over the bottom. Use just enough batter to make a very thin

18

pancake. Cook on medium-high heat until batter congeals—bottom should not brown. Slide out onto a platter, stacking cakes bottom side up as you make them. When all 8 blintzes are cooked, fill them, using ½ cup Cheese Filling for each. Spread filling along one edge of cooked side of pancake; tuck sides in and roll up, starting with the side that is spread with filling. Refrigerate until ready to serve. Brown blintzes in butter in a skillet over medium heat, turning once, adding butter as needed.

CHEESE FILLING

4 **cups well-drained small-curd cottage cheese or pot cheese**
2 **egg yolks**

¼ **cup sugar**
2 **tablespoons lemon juice**

Combine all ingredients in a small bowl, stirring until well blended.
Helpful to know: Blintzes freeze well.
Idea: If you prefer, bake the blintzes, instead of sautéing them, in a well-buttered casserole in a preheated 425° oven until browned.

BASIL TOMATOES   8 servings

3 **to 4 beefsteak tomatoes**
¼ **cup olive oil**
3 **tablespoons wine vinegar**
  Sugar

2 **teaspoons crumbled basil**
  Salt and freshly ground
  black pepper to taste

Cut tomatoes into ¼-inch slices. Lay slices, slightly overlapping, in an attractive pattern on a serving platter. Mix oil, vinegar and pinch of sugar. Sprinkle over tomatoes. Sprinkle with basil, then with salt and finish with a few grindings of pepper. Refrigerate at least 1 hour.

BREAKFAST CAKE   12 servings

½ **cup butter, softened**
¾ **cup sugar**
1 **teaspoon vanilla extract**
3 **eggs**
2 **cups sifted flour**
1 **teaspoon baking powder**

1 **teaspoon baking soda**
1 **cup dairy sour cream**
6 **tablespoons butter, softened**
1 **cup dark brown sugar, firmly packed**
2 **teaspoons cinnamon**
1 **cup chopped pecans**

Cream butter, sugar and vanilla thoroughly. Add eggs, 1 at a time, beating well after each addition. Sift flour, baking powder and baking soda together. Add to creamed mixture alternately with sour cream, blending after each addition. Spread half of batter in a 10-inch tube pan that has been oiled and lined on the bottom with waxed paper. Cream butter, brown sugar and cinnamon together. Add nuts; mix well. Sprinkle half of nut mixture evenly over batter in pan. Cover with remaining batter; sprinkle on remaining nut mixture. Bake in a preheated 350° oven for about 50 minutes, or until done.

BRUNCH IT YOURSELF

Here are more good-for-brunch dishes—around which you can build your own, suit-yourself brunch menus.

SMIRNOFF ROYAL ADE
1 drink

Juice of 1 lemon
Juice of 1 lime
1 tablespoon confectioners sugar

2 ounces Smirnoff Vodka
¼ teaspoon grenadine
Carbonated water

Shake fruit juices, sugar, vodka and grenadine well with cracked ice. Strain into a tall collins glass. Fill with carbonated water. If desired, decorate with a cherry and a slice of fruit.

SMIRNOFF STORMCLOUD
1 drink

1 ounce Smirnoff Vodka
1 ounce Arrow Brown Crème de Cacao

½ ounce lemon juice
Dash grenadine

Shake all ingredients well with cracked ice. Strain into a 3-ounce cocktail glass.

SMIRNOFF AND APPLE JUICE
1 drink

2 ounces Smirnoff Vodka

Apple juice

Put 2 or 3 ice cubes into a 6-ounce glass. Add vodka; fill glass with apple juice. Stir.

SMIRNOFF GRASSHOPPER
1 drink

¾ ounce Smirnoff Vodka
¾ ounce Arrow White Crème de Cacao

½ ounce Arrow Crème de Menthe

Shake ingredients well with cracked ice. Strain into a 3-ounce cocktail glass.

EGGS IN NOODLE NESTS
6 servings

1 anchovy fillet
10 tablespoons butter, divided
4 cups cooked fine noodles
6 chicken livers, broiled and chopped
6 eggs
1 cup milk

1 bay leaf
Salt and pepper to taste
1 tablespoon flour
½ cup heavy cream
½ cup grated Gruyère cheese

Blend anchovy into a paste with 4 tablespoons butter; melt. Butter 6 individual casseroles with this anchovy butter. Melt 2 tablespoons butter and toss with noodles. Line casseroles with noodles. Place one-sixth of the chopped chicken liver in each nest of noodles. Break an egg into center of

21

nest. Bake in a preheated 350° oven for 5 minutes, or until egg just begins to set. Remove from oven. Heat milk with bay leaf and seasonings. Remove bay leaf. Melt 1 tablespoon butter in a saucepan; combine with flour and cook until bubbling. Stir in strained milk. Bring to a boil; reduce over medium heat by a third. Stir in cream and cheese until melted. Stir in 3 tablespoons butter. Pour 3 tablespoons sauce over each egg nest. Place casseroles on baking sheet and broil a few moments, or until lightly browned.

CURRIED EGGS AND CHESTNUTS
6 servings

3 cups boiled chestnuts	½ teaspoon salt
3 tablespoons butter	Paprika
3 tablespoons flour	6 hard-cooked eggs (page 137),
1½ cups light cream	shelled and quartered
½ cup grated Cheddar cheese	½ cup buttered bread crumbs
1 teaspoon curry powder	

Quarter chestnuts if large, otherwise leave whole. Melt butter in a saucepan; blend in flour. Add cream slowly, stirring continuously for 5 minutes. Add cheese and seasonings; cool 2 minutes. Divide eggs and chestnuts among 6 individual baking dishes. Add sauce; sprinkle with bread crumbs. Brown under moderate broiler flame. Serve at once.
Helpful to know: You can buy canned, cooked, water-packed chestnuts.

EGGS EN CROUTE
4 servings

4 thick slices French	4 eggs
or Italian bread	Salt and pepper to taste
½ cup melted butter	1 cup cheese sauce or tomato sauce

Scoop a small hollow out of center of each bread slice and discard. Dip each slice in melted butter and place on baking sheet. Break an egg into each hollow. Sprinkle with salt and pepper. Bake in a preheated 325° oven until eggs are set. Serve with hot sauce.

EGG FRITTERS
6 servings

1½ cups sifted flour	12 hard-cooked eggs (page 137),
2 teaspoons baking powder	shelled and chopped
½ teaspoon salt	1 tablespoon grated onion
1 egg	2 teaspoons finely snipped parsley
1 egg yolk	Salt and pepper to taste
⅔ cup light cream,	Oil or shortening for deep-fat frying
scalded and cooled	

Sift flour, baking powder and salt into a bowl. Beat whole egg, yolk and cream together. Beat in flour mixture gradually, stirring until smooth. Stir in chopped eggs, onion, parsley and seasonings; mix gently. Let stand 5 minutes. Drop from a teaspoon into 1 inch of hot oil. Fry until golden on both sides. Drain. Serve at once with desired sauce.

POACHED EGGS IN WHITE WINE

4 servings

3 tablespoons butter
¾ cup dry white wine
4 eggs
Salt and pepper to taste

Paprika
4 teaspoons grated Roquefort cheese
4 slices hot buttered toast

Heat butter in a skillet over low heat. Stir in wine. Place 4 individual ring molds into wine. Break an egg into center of each ring. Season to taste and poach over low heat. Baste frequently with wine-butter mixture until eggs are nearly set. Sprinkle with cheese and continue poaching until cheese has melted. Serve at once on toast.

CORN FRITTERS

16 fritters

1 cup canned cream-style corn
2 eggs, beaten
6 tablespoons flour

½ teaspoon baking powder
¼ teaspoon salt
3 tablespoons butter

Place corn in a mixing bowl; add eggs. Mix in flour, baking powder and salt. Melt butter in a skillet over medium heat. Drop in the batter by table-spoonfuls. Brown fritters on first side, then turn and brown second side. Serve at once with syrup, if desired.

CONTINENTAL SALAD

8 servings

2 small hearts of celery
2 small heads Boston lettuce
1 avocado, peeled, pitted and diced

¼ cup diced pimiento
½ cup French Dressing (page 87)

Cut celery into ¼-inch crosswise slices; place in salad bowl. Add lettuce, torn into pieces, avocado and pimiento. Just before serving, pour on dressing and toss.
Try this way: Crumble 2 tablespoons bleu cheese over salad before pouring on dressing.

CHICKEN-SALAD MOLLET

4 servings

1 cup mayonnaise
½ teaspoon dry mustard
1 teaspoon lemon juice
Salt and white pepper to taste
2 cups diced, cooked chicken
½ cup diced celery

1 head Boston lettuce,
separated into leaves
4 Eggs Mollet (page 138)
3 slices cooked beef tongue,
slivered
6 ripe olives, pitted and chopped

Combine mayonnaise, mustard, lemon juice and dash each of salt and pepper. Pour over combined chicken and celery; mix lightly. Arrange lettuce in a bowl or a serving plate. Mound chicken salad in center and place eggs on salad. Sprinkle with the tongue and the olives.

BELGIAN TURKEY

8 servings

6 tablespoons butter
8 heads Belgian endive
2 cups (about) chicken broth

2 jars (1 pound each) cheese sauce
Milk
8 large slices cooked turkey

In a large skillet, melt butter and brown endive in it on all sides over fairly high heat. Add chicken broth—use just enough to cover the bottom of the pan well. Cover and simmer 15 minutes, adding more broth if necessary; there should be almost no broth left when endive is done. While endive is cooking, heat cheese sauce with enough milk to thin to a heavy pouring consistency. Oil a large, shallow casserole. Place turkey in casserole and place a head of endive on each slice. Pour sauce over. Brown under broiler for about 3 minutes.

LITTLE COCONUT TARTS

4 dozens

1⅓ cups sifted flour
⅓ cup sugar
¼ teaspoon salt
¾ cup butter

1 egg, slightly beaten
1 egg
1 can (3½ ounces) flaked coconut
⅔ cup sugar

Sift flour with ⅓ cup sugar and the salt into a medium-size bowl. With pastry blender, cut in butter until mixture resembles coarse crumbs. With a fork, stir in the beaten egg. Knead slightly until mixture holds together. Wrap in waxed paper; refrigerate several hours, or until firm. With fork, beat egg in small bowl. Add coconut and ⅔ cup sugar; mix well. For each tart, pinch off about 1 teaspoon chilled dough. Press into 2- x ½-inch tart pan to make a shell ⅛ inch thick. Fill each shell with 1 teaspoon filling. Set tarts on cookie sheet. Bake in preheated 375° oven for 12 minutes, or until coconut filling is golden brown. Place pans on wire rack; cool slightly. With small spatula, gently remove tarts from pans.

CHOCOLATE COFFEE ROLL

8 to 10 servings

1 envelope or cake yeast,
  active dry or compressed
2½ cups sifted flour
½ cup cocoa
1¼ cups sugar

¼ teaspoon salt
¼ cup butter
3 eggs
Filling

Oil a cookie sheet. Dissolve the yeast in ¼ cup warm (105°-115°) water. Sift the flour, cocoa, sugar and salt together. Cut in the butter with a pastry blender. Add the eggs, 1 at a time, beating well after each addition. Add the dissolved yeast and beat again. Put in an oiled bowl and turn once to bring oiled side up. Cover and let rise in a warm place, free from draft, until doubled in bulk, about 2 hours. In the meantime, make Filling.

FILLING

2 squares (1 ounce each) unsweetened chocolate, melted
2 tablespoons brandy
½ cup honey
2 cups filberts, ground
½ cup dried currants

Mix ingredients thoroughly. When the dough has risen, roll it out into an oblong about ½ inch thick. Spread with the filling and roll like a jelly roll. Place on cookie sheet. Bake in a preheated 375° oven for 25 minutes.

COLD WINE CUSTARD   6 servings

6 egg yolks
6 tablespoons sugar
½ cup sweet Marsala wine
1 cup heavy cream
6 maraschino cherries

Beat yolks in electric mixer until blended. Continue beating while adding the sugar a tablespoon at a time. Add wine gradually. Place mixture in top of a double boiler. Cook over boiling water, stirring constantly until thickened, 3 to 4 minutes. Cool. Whip cream until stiff; fold in cooled custard. Spoon into serving dishes, top with maraschino cherries; refrigerate.

ANGEL FOOD CAKE   12 servings

1¼ cups (about 10 to 12) egg whites
1 cup plus 2 tablespoons sifted cake flour
1½ cups sugar, divided
½ teaspoon salt
1¼ teaspoons cream of tartar
1 teaspoon vanilla extract
¼ teaspoon almond extract

Let egg whites stand at room temperature about 1 hour. Sift together flour and 1 cup of the sugar 4 times. Reserve. In large bowl of electric mixer combine egg whites and remaining ingredients. Beat at highest speed until egg whites are stiff and form soft peaks, 1½ to 2 minutes. Do not overbeat. Turn to medium speed and beat while gradually adding remaining sugar. Beat until sugar is just blended. Turn to lowest speed. Sprinkle in sifted flour mixture evenly and quickly, scraping up and over with a folding motion, only until blended, about 1½ minutes. Remove bowl and fold batter, folding over and over a few times with a rubber scraper. Carefully spoon batter into an unoiled 10-inch tube pan. Cut through batter with a spatula, going around in widening circles 6 times without lifting spatula. Bake in a preheated 375° oven for 30 to 35 minutes, or until a cake tester inserted comes out clean. Remove from oven and invert tube on the neck of a bottle at once; let hang upside down until completely cold.

PECAN LOG   12 servings

5 ounces (about) shelled pecans
1 teaspoon baking powder
6 eggs, separated
¾ cup sugar
2 cups heavy cream
1 teaspoon vanilla extract
2 tablespoons sugar

Whirl pecans in blender to make 1½ cups, chopped very finely. Mix in baking powder and reserve. Beat egg whites until they form stiff peaks. Reserve. Add ¾ cup sugar to yolks and beat until thick and pale yellow. Fold in pecan mixture. Fold yolk mixture into whites. Oil a 15½- x 10½- x 1-inch jelly-roll pan; line bottom with waxed paper. Pour in batter and spread evenly. Bake in a preheated 350° oven for 20 to 30 minutes, or until cake starts to pull away from sides of pan. Leave cake in pan, cover with a damp towel and refrigerate. About 1 hour before serving, whip cream, add vanilla and 2 tablespoons sugar. Turn cake over onto damp towel and remove pan. Peel off paper. Trim off crusty edges. Spread whipped cream on cake and roll from long side like a jelly roll. Refrigerate. Slice and serve.
Idea: This may be served plain or with additional whipped cream or with crushed and sweetened strawberries.

WHITE FRUITCAKE
3 loaves

1 cup butter, softened
2 cups sugar
7 eggs, separated
3 cups sifted flour
3 teaspoons baking powder
⅛ teaspoon salt
1 can (13½ ounces) crushed pineapple

Flour
2 pounds golden raisins
1 pound mixed candied fruit
½ pound blanched almonds, chopped
1 teaspoon vanilla extract
1 teaspoon almond extract

Cream the butter and sugar thoroughly in a large mixing bowl; add egg yolks, 1 at a time, beating well after each addition. Add combined and sifted dry ingredients alternately with the pineapple juice drained from crushed pineapple. Sprinkle a little flour over the raisins, mixed fruit and nuts; then add to creamed mixture alternately with the crushed pineapple, blending thoroughly. Add flavorings. Beat egg whites until stiff but not dry; fold into batter. Line 3 medium-size oiled and floured loaf pans with waxed paper; then oil the paper. Pour in the batter. Bake in a preheated 300° oven until a cake tester inserted in the center comes out clean—about 3 hours. Turn out on wire racks and remove waxed paper. Let cool thoroughly before storing in an airtight metal container.

BRUNCH FOR TWO

BEDROOM BRUNCH

Brunch for two should be very special. It's the one time of the week when you are free from business worries, away from people of the work-aday world—you're alone in your own castle. On the day you wake up remembering that your husband has had a particularly hard week, you think, "I'll make something special for brunch and serve him in bed." The something special is delectable Onion Quiche. The bacon cooks while the quiche bakes. Buy the dilled green beans in a jar. Brown-and-serve croissants need only a brief time in the oven while the coffee perks. Start the brunch with an eye-opening Smirnoff Bloody Bullshot or a Smirnoff White Russian or a Smirnoff Salty Dog—and bring along all the Sunday papers to peruse at leisure.

Smirnoff Bloody Bullshots or Smirnoff White Russians
or Smirnoff Salty Dogs
Onion Quiche   Grilled Canadian Bacon
Hot Croissants   Wild-Cherry Preserve
Dilled Green Beans
Coffee

SMIRNOFF BLOODY BULLSHOT   1 drink

1 ounce Smirnoff Vodka   **2 ounces tomato juice**
½ ounce beef bouillon   **Dash of lemon**

Combine vodka, bouillon, tomato juice and lemon in a double old-fashioned glass. Add ice cubes and stir.

SMIRNOFF WHITE RUSSIAN   1 drink

1 ounce Smirnoff Vodka   **1 ounce milk**
¾ ounce coffee liqueur

Pour each ingredient separately over ice cubes in a 6-ounce glass. Provide stirrers, but do not stir until just before drinking.

SMIRNOFF SALTY DOG

1 drink

1 ounce Smirnoff Vodka
2 ounces unsweetened grapefruit juice

1 ounce orange juice
Dash of salt

Place vodka, grapefruit juice, orange juice and salt in a glass with 2 or 3 ice cubes. Stir.

ONION QUICHE

2 servings

1 7-inch pastry shell
3 tablespoons butter
⅓ cup chopped onion
¾ cup grated Swiss cheese
3 eggs, beaten

1 teaspoon Grey Poupon mustard
¼ teaspoon salt
Sprinkle of cayenne
1¼ cups scalded milk

Buy a frozen pastry shell or make your own. Melt butter and cook onion in it until soft but not browned; spoon onion and butter into bottom of pastry shell. Cover with cheese. To eggs, add mustard, salt and cayenne. Slowly pour in scalded milk, stirring constantly. Pour this mixture over the cheese. Bake in a preheated 375° oven for 30 minutes, or until browned.

IT'S A SPECIAL THING

For you, it's a long, lazy, the-two-of-us summer day to relax in. But the man in your life wants to watch baseball on TV—and the doubleheader starts early. What are you going to do? Sulk? Offer him a sandwich and a soda? No, you're going to fix such a scrumptious, serve-it-at-the-television brunch that he'll savor every bite and miss the big plays because he's so busy complimenting you.

Smirnoff Screwdrivers (see page 17)
Baked Bacon   Eggs Florentine
Toasted French Bread   Cream Twists
Fresh Strawberries   Coffee

BAKED BACON

2 servings

6 slices thick-sliced raw bacon

Lay bacon slices on rack of bacon baker or on a rack set in a baking pan. Bake in a preheated 400° oven until done to your liking.
Try this way: If you prefer, bacon may be breaded with flour, beaten egg and cracker crumbs, and baked in the same manner.

EGGS FLORENTINE

2 servings

1 package (10½ ounces) frozen
   chopped spinach
1 tablespoon butter
2 tablespoons minced onion

Salt and pepper to taste
4 eggs
¼ cup light cream

Cook spinach according to package directions and drain thoroughly. Melt butter in small skillet. Add onion and cook gently until soft but not browned. Toss onion and butter with spinach. Season with salt and pepper. Butter 2 individual casseroles. Divide spinach between them. Break 2 eggs on top of each spinach bed. Pour 1 tablespoon cream over each egg. Season lightly. Bake in preheated 350° oven until eggs are set to your liking.

CREAM TWISTS

20 pastries

4 cups sifted flour
1 teaspoon salt
1 cup butter
1 package or cake yeast,
   active dry or compressed
1 egg

2 egg yolks
1 cup dairy sour cream
2 teaspoons vanilla extract
½ teaspoon nutmeg
Sugar

Sift flour and salt into a bowl. With a pastry blender or two knives, cut in butter until mixture is the consistency of coarse bread crumbs. Measure ¼ cup warm (105°-115°) water into a small bowl. Add yeast and stir until dissolved. Beat together egg, egg yolks and sour cream. Add yeast, vanilla and nutmeg. Add egg mixture to flour-butter mixture and blend thoroughly. Refrigerate for 2 hours. At the end of that time, lightly sprinkle sugar on a board, place the dough on the board and sprinkle with more sugar. Roll out to a 12-inch square and fold dough from each side to the middle. Roll and repeat 4 times in all, using more sugar as necessary to keep dough from sticking to rolling pin. Cut into strips ¾ inch wide by 4 inches long. Sprinkle with sugar and twist each strip. Place on unoiled cookie sheet several inches apart. Bake in a preheated 375° oven about 20 minutes, or until lightly browned. Store closely covered.
Helpful to know: These pastries require no rising time other than that spent in the refrigerator.

SWEETER THAN SPRINGTIME

Spring is in the air. You know what a young man's fancy turns to—and a young lady's fancy turns to thoughts of foods to please her man. The fresh early spring asparagus, with a touch of lemon butter. The pinkest of strawberries nestled in a ring of palest orange. And best of all, the king of brunches, Eggs Benedict smothered in Hollandaise Sauce. While he's drooling over the goodies to come, calm his hunger pangs with a Smirnoff Milk Punch.

Smirnoff Milk Punch
Eggs Benedict   Asparagus with Lemon Butter
Fresh Strawberries in Soufflé Ring
Coffee

SMIRNOFF MILK PUNCH

1 drink

1 teaspoon confectioners sugar
2 ounces Smirnoff Vodka

1 cup milk
1 ounce Arrow Peppermint Schnapps

Combine all ingredients and shake well with cracked ice. Strain into a tall glass and sprinkle with grated nutmeg, if desired.

EGGS BENEDICT

2 servings

2 English muffins, split
  Butter
4 slices ham, sautéed

4 poached eggs (page 138)
  Hollandaise Sauce

Toast and butter English muffins and place 2 halves on each serving plate. Top each with a slice of ham, then with a poached egg. Spoon Hollandaise Sauce over each egg and serve at once.

HOLLANDAISE SAUCE

1 cup

3 egg yolks
2 tablespoons lemon juice
  Sprinkle of cayenne

¼ teaspoon salt
⅔ cup butter

Place yolks, lemon juice and seasonings in blender container. Melt butter to bubbling stage, but do not brown. Cover blender and turn to high speed; after 3 seconds remove cover and pour the butter over in a thin, steady stream. Sauce will be finished in 30 to 35 seconds. Keep warm by immersing blender container in warm water.

SOUFFLE RING

6 servings

3 tablespoons butter, softened
⅓ cup flour
¾ cup hot milk
¼ teaspoon salt
⅓ cup sugar
1 tablespoon frozen orange
  juice concentrate, undiluted

1 teaspoon grated orange peel
½ teaspoon almond extract
4 egg whites, stiffly
  beaten
  Sliced, sweetened strawberries

With heat off, cream butter in top of double boiler. Add flour and mix until smooth. Add hot milk gradually; cook over boiling water, stirring constantly, until mixture comes away from sides of pan. Remove from heat. Add salt, sugar, juice, peel and extract. Fold in egg whites. Oil and flour a ring mold on the bottom only. Turn mixture into mold, set in a pan of hot water and bake in preheated 350° oven 45 minutes. Cool 5 minutes; turn out on a serving plate. Chill. To serve, fill center with strawberries.

LIVE A LITTLE

Grandmother has the kids for the weekend, so indulge yourselves with brunch for just the two of you. Make it festive—start with a Smirnoff Bloody Mary. Make it fit for a king and use the very best ingredients— the plumpest, ripest, perfumiest pears from the greengrocer, the mellowest wedge of Brie the cheese store can produce.

Smirnoff Bloody Marys (see page 9)
Cloud Eggs   Brunch Kabobs
Best-Ever Biscuits   Honey
Fresh Pears   Brie   Coffee

CLOUD EGGS
2 servings

4 slices thin-sliced white bread	4 eggs
Snipped parsley	¼ teaspoon salt
	Dash of white pepper

Toast bread lightly and butter on one side. Sprinkle buttered side with parsley. Separate eggs, keeping yolks whole. Beat whites until stiff but not dry. Season with salt and pepper. Mound the beaten whites on the toast slices. With a spoon, carefully lift egg yolks and press into whites. Bake in a preheated 475° oven for 4 to 6 minutes, or until egg whites are lightly browned.

BRUNCH KABOBS
2 servings

4 slices raw bacon	8 cherry tomatoes
8 mushrooms	8 chunks green pepper

Cut bacon into squares. Wipe off mushrooms with a damp paper towel. Wash tomatoes and dry. Thread on 4 short skewers in this manner: bacon, tomato, bacon, pepper, bacon, mushroom—repeat. Broil until bacon is crisp, turning frequently.

BEST-EVER BISCUITS
about 2 dozens

1¾ cups sifted flour	6 tablespoons cold butter
1 teaspoon salt	⅔ cup milk
2 teaspoons baking powder	

Sift together dry ingredients into a bowl. With two knives or a pastry blender, cut in butter until the mixture is the consistency of coarse cornmeal. Add milk all at once and stir briefly until dough leaves the side of the bowl. Turn dough out on a floured board and knead gently and quickly about 30 seconds. Pat out dough to about ½-inch thickness. Cut with a biscuit cutter dipped into a very little flour and place on a lightly oiled baking sheet. Brush tops of biscuits with milk and bake in a preheated 450° oven for 12 to 15 minutes.

Helpful to know: If you place biscuits on sheet with sides touching, they will be soft; if you place each separately, they will be crusty—have them the way you like them best.

OYSTERS "R" IN SEASON

Serve the man in your life Oysters Suprême, a relative (not as close as kissing cousins) of Oysters Rockefeller. They're easy to put together when you serve them with the brunch planned here. You'll both feel like millionaires.

Smirnoff Sours
Oysters Suprême　*Swiss-broiled Tomatoes*
Popovers　*Ginger Conserve*
Apples and Camembert　*Coffee*

SMIRNOFF SOUR
1 drink

2 ounces Smirnoff Vodka
1 tablespoon lemon juice
½ teaspoon sugar

½ cup crushed ice
Lime slice
Fresh pineapple stick

Combine vodka, lemon juice, sugar and ice in the container of a blender. Cover and process at low speed 1 minute. Pour into sours glass. Garnish with a lime slice and a small stick of fresh pineapple.

OYSTERS SUPREME
2 servings

1 package (10½ ounces) frozen
chopped spinach
2 tablespoons butter
2 tablespoons chopped onion
2 teaspoons lemon juice

Salt and pepper to taste
Few grains of nutmeg
2 English muffins
12 large oysters
4 slices raw bacon

Cook spinach according to package directions; drain well. Melt butter in skillet; cook onion in butter until soft but not browned. Add spinach, lemon juice, salt, pepper and nutmeg; mix lightly. Split and toast English muffins. Divide spinach mixture over the 4 muffin halves. Place 3 oysters on each muffin half. Cut bacon slices in half; fry until nearly done, and crisscross 2 bacon strips over each. Broil until bacon is crisp and edges of oysters are curled. Serve at once.

SWISS-BROILED TOMATOES
2 servings

2 small, ripe tomatoes
Salt and white pepper to taste
2 tablespoons fine, dry
   bread crumbs

½ teaspoon basil
2 teaspoons melted butter
¼ cup grated Swiss cheese

Cut tomatoes in half. Season lightly with salt and pepper. Mix remaining ingredients and pile lightly on tomato halves. Broil, along with the Oysters Suprême, until cheese begins to melt and topping is lightly browned.

POPOVERS
9 popovers

1 cup milk
1 tablespoon melted butter
1 cup flour

¼ teaspoon salt
2 eggs

Lightly oil 9 deep muffin tins or custard cups. Beat milk, butter, flour and salt together until just smooth. Add eggs 1 at a time, beating after each just enough to combine it with the milk mixture. Fill muffin tins no more than three-quarters full. Bake in a preheated 450° oven for 15 minutes. Lower heat to 350° (don't peek at the popovers) and bake about 20 minutes longer. Insert a sharp paring knife lightly into each popover to allow steam to escape. Serve at once.

SUNLIGHT AND ROSES

Can't set a romantic table for two without darkness and candlelight? Yes, you can! Place a small table on the terrace or patio; get out that damask cloth your aunt left you; use your best china, crystal and silver. And serve a meal guaranteed to make the man melt!

Smirnoff Yellow Fevers
Chive-Cheese Eggs   Broiled Ham Steaks
Pecan Buttermilk Muffins
San Diego Oranges   Coffee

SMIRNOFF YELLOW FEVER

1 drink

1 teaspoon sugar
  Juice of ½ lemon

2 ounces Smirnoff Vodka
  Water or club soda

Dissolve sugar in lemon juice in bottom of 8-ounce glass. Add vodka and ice cubes. Fill with water or club soda.

CHIVE-CHEESE EGGS

2 servings

4 eggs
  Salt and white pepper to taste
1 package (3 ounces)
  chived cream cheese

2 tablespoons butter

Break eggs into a small bowl, season with salt and pepper and beat lightly. Cut cheese into cubes. Melt butter in a small, heavy skillet. Add eggs and cook over very low heat until just beginning to set. Sprinkle cheese cubes over eggs and continue to cook just until eggs are softly set and cheese is melted.

PECAN BUTTERMILK MUFFINS

2 dozens

2 cups sifted cake flour
1 teaspoon baking powder
½ teaspoon salt
2 tablespoons sugar
½ teaspoon baking soda

1 cup buttermilk
3 tablespoons melted butter
1 egg, beaten
½ cup chopped pecans

Sift together dry ingredients. Combine buttermilk, butter and egg. Add milk mixture all at once to dry ingredients. Add pecans and mix only enough to combine. Do not beat. Mixture will be slightly lumpy. Fill well-oiled muffin tins two-thirds full. Bake in a preheated 400° oven 20 to 25 minutes, or until muffins are puffed and lightly browned.
Helpful to know: Reheat leftover muffins, loosely wrapped in aluminum foil, in a preheated 450° oven for 5 minutes.

SAN DIEGO ORANGES

2 servings

2 large navel oranges
¼ cup dairy sour cream

¼ cup light brown
  sugar, firmly packed

Peel oranges, being careful to remove all white membrane, and slice very thinly with a sharp knife. Arrange on 2 serving plates. Place a mound of sour cream on each plate. Sprinkle with brown sugar.
Try this way: Substitute maple sugar for the brown sugar—wonderful!

BRUNCH IT YOURSELF

Here are more good-for-brunch dishes—around which you can build your own, suit-yourself brunch menus.

SMIRNOFF AND CHERRY   1 drink

1½ ounces Smirnoff Vodka   Juice of ½ lime
¾ ounce Cherry Heering   Twist of lime peel

With cracked ice, shake vodka, Cherry Heering and lime juice. Serve in a chilled champagne glass with the lime peel.

SMIRNOFF SUMMER MARTINI   1 drink

2 ounces Smirnoff Vodka   Lime wedge
  Club soda

Pour vodka over ice cubes in an old-fashioned glass. Fill with club soda. Stir. Serve with lime wedge.

CANTALOUPE WITH STRAWBERRY SAUCE   2 servings

½ cup fresh strawberries,   1½ tablespoons lemon juice
  washed and hulled   1 small cantaloupe,
2 tablespoons sugar   halved and seeded

Mash the strawberries or whirl in blender. Add sugar and lemon juice, cover and process a few moments longer. Pour sauce into the 2 halves of cantaloupe; cover and chill in refrigerator until serving time (at least 1 hour).

SHAD-ROE OMELET   2 servings

2 tablespoons butter   Dash of pepper
½ cup cooked roe, lightly mashed ¼ cup milk
½ teaspoon onion juice   6 eggs
½ teaspoon salt

Melt butter in large skillet; add roe, onion juice, salt and pepper. Stir gently until heated. Add milk and 2 tablespoons water to eggs; beat lightly. Pour into pan with roe. Draw edges of mixture to center until eggs are set. Serve at once, folded in half, on warm platter.

LOBSTER OMELET   2 servings

4 eggs, separated   Dash of pepper
½ cup milk   ¼ teaspoon salt
1 cup lobster meat, cut in chunks ⅛ teaspoon dry mustard
1 teaspoon finely snipped parsley 6 tablespoons butter

Beat egg yolks. Combine with milk, lobster and seasonings. Beat egg whites until stiff but not dry in separate bowl. Fold yolk mixture into egg whites. Melt butter in omelet pan. Pour in egg mixture and cook slowly until set. Place under low broiler to set top. Fold in half. Serve at once.

PICARDY OMELET

2 servings

1 cup canned tomatoes, drained
2 tablespoons butter
2 small onions, minced
1 small clove garlic, minced
2 tablespoons fresh bread crumbs

1 tablespoon minced green pepper
Salt and pepper to taste
Dash cayenne
4 eggs, separated

Mash tomatoes to a pulp in small bowl. Melt butter in a skillet. Add onions, garlic, bread crumbs and green pepper. Sauté until brown. Add tomatoes, salt, pepper and cayenne; simmer 15 to 20 minutes. Beat egg yolks lightly. Beat egg whites until stiff but not dry; fold into yolks. Melt enough butter in a second skillet to coat the bottom; add egg mixture. Cook over low heat, shaking skillet gently while mixture sets. Pour tomato mixture over the eggs; cook 2 minutes longer. Fold in half and serve at once.

ARTICHOKE OMELET

2 servings

4 large cooked artichoke
  hearts, minced
1 tablespoon butter
⅓ cup Béchamel Sauce
5 eggs, beaten

Salt and pepper to taste
1 tablespoon butter
Small triangles of bread,
  fried in butter
Watercress

Sauté artichokes in 1 tablespoon butter. Mix with 4 tablespoons sauce. Season beaten eggs with salt and pepper. Melt 1 tablespoon butter in omelet pan; pour in eggs. Shake and stir with flat fork until set to your liking. When omelet is ready for folding, place artichoke mixture in center. Fold omelet, slide onto a hot platter and spread with remainder of sauce. Serve on bread triangles and garnish with watercress.

BECHAMEL SAUCE

2 tablespoons butter
3 tablespoons flour
2 cups milk or white stock

¼ teaspoon salt
1 bay leaf

Melt butter in saucepan. Blend in flour and cook, slowly stirring, until bubbling. Remove from heat. Heat milk with salt and bay leaf in another saucepan and let stand for 1 minute. Remove bay leaf. Gradually add milk to flour mixture, stirring constantly. Beat until smooth. Bring to a boil and cook for 1 minute, stirring constantly.

THE CELEBRATION BRUNCH

A DAY IN MAY

The first day, to be precise—and it is worthy of celebration. You don't need to go so far as to exchange May baskets or stage a Maypole dance, but after an appropriate-for-May brunch you might shoo everyone outdoors to do as he sees fit—the exercise-minded to play lawn games, the cerebral to set up a card game in a secluded corner, the frankly lazy just to sit and exchange ideas all afternoon.

Smirnoff Plum Punch
Watercress Soup
Caraway Crackers
Lobster Crepes   Crepes Ratatouille
Sweet Gherkins
Whole Fresh Strawberries Dipped in Confectioners Sugar
Butter Cookies   Coffee

SMIRNOFF PLUM PUNCH
25 drinks

2 jars (12 ounces each) plum jelly
2 cans (6 ounces each) frozen orange juice concentrate, undiluted
½ cup lemon juice

6 bottles (7 ounces each) lemon-lime soda
2 cups Smirnoff Vodka

Beat jelly until smooth. Gradually beat in 2 cups boiling water, mixing until smooth. Blend in orange juice. Chill mixture until cold. Combine jelly mixture and lemon juice over ice cubes in a punch bowl. Slowly add lemon-lime beverage and vodka. Stir gently.

WATERCRESS SOUP
6 to 8 servings

1 cup watercress leaves, washed
1 small cucumber, peeled, seeded and cut in pieces
1 can (10½ ounces) condensed cream of asparagus soup

1½ cups milk
¼ teaspoon salt
½ cup light cream

Combine all ingredients, except the cream, in blender container. Cover and process until smooth. Stir in the cream and chill.

CREPES

1 cup plus 2 tablespoons
   sifted flour
   Pinch of salt
3 eggs, beaten

1½ cups milk
 1 tablespoon melted butter
1½ tablespoons Cognac (optional)
 ¼ cup butter, divided

Combine flour and salt in a bowl. Beat eggs and milk together. Stir into flour mixture and beat until smooth. This can be done on low speed of a mixer or with a wire whisk. Stir in melted butter and Cognac. Let mixture stand at least 2 hours before cooking. Heat a crepe pan, about 5½ inches in diameter across the bottom, over medium-high heat. When skillet is hot, add ½ teaspoon butter and swirl around pan to cover sides and bottom. Pour in 1 full tablespoon batter. Rotate and tilt pan quickly to spread batter evenly over bottom of skillet. This must be done quickly before batter has a chance to set. Cook crepe about 1 minute, or until it is set and brown on one side. Loosen sides with a spatula and flip crepe over quickly with the fingers. Lightly brown second side. Since the second side will not brown as nicely as the first side, it is usually turned inside when it is rolled around a filling. Stack crepes in a pile as they are cooked. They may be used immediately or made early in the day and filled just before serving. *Idea:* These crepes may also be frozen, using pieces of waxed paper to separate the crepes from one another.

LOBSTER CREPES

1 cup sliced fresh mushrooms *or* 1 can
   (4 ounces) sliced mushrooms,
   drained
½ cup chopped scallions
¼ cup diced pimiento
¼ cup butter
1½ cups diced, cooked lobster meat
 3 tablespoons butter

 3 tablespoons flour
 ½ teaspoon salt
 ¼ teaspoon pepper
 1 bottle (8 ounces) clam juice
 ½ cup dry white wine
 2 egg yolks
 ½ cup heavy cream
12 crepes

Sauté mushrooms, scallions and pimiento in ¼ cup hot butter. Cook over low heat for 5 minutes, or until onion is soft but not browned. Stir in lobster meat and remove from heat. Melt 3 tablespoons butter in another saucepan. Stir in flour, salt and pepper. Remove from heat and stir in clam juice and wine. Cook, stirring constantly, until sauce thickens and comes to a boil. Simmer gently 1 minute. Beat egg yolks with heavy cream. Stir a little of the hot sauce into the egg yolks. Blend well. Return egg mixture to hot sauce in saucepan and blend thoroughly. Cook over low heat, stirring constantly, 2 minutes. Remove from heat. Mix 1 cup of the hot sauce into reserved lobster mixture. Spoon about 2 tablespoons of the lobster filling in a band down center of each crepe. Fold both sides up over the filling. Place, folded side up, in a single layer in a lightly oiled, shallow baking dish. Pour remaining wine sauce over top of crepes. Bake in a preheated 400° oven for 15 minutes, or until sauce is bubbly around edges.

CREPES RATATOUILLE

6 servings

1 eggplant, about 1 pound	2 cloves garlic, crushed
1½ teaspoons salt	2 teaspoons salt
2 green peppers	1 teaspoon pepper
2 tomatoes	1 tablespoon basil
2 medium-size zucchini	1 teaspoon rosemary
2 tablespoons salad oil	1 teaspoon marjoram
2 tablespoons butter	12 crepes
2 small onions, sliced	Butter, melted

Cut unpeeled eggplant into ½-inch-thick slices. Sprinkle with 1½ teaspoons of the salt. Place eggplant on a paper-towel-lined jelly-roll pan. Cover slices with more paper towels. Place several weights on top and let press for 30 minutes. Halve the green peppers and remove seeds. Slice lengthwise into ¼-inch-wide strips. Cut tomatoes in half and remove seeds. Dice remaining pulp. Slice zucchini into ¼-inch-thick slices. Remove eggplant from paper towels and cut into small cubes. In a large skillet heat the salad oil and butter. Add onions and garlic and cook 5 minutes, or until tender and lightly browned. Add green pepper strips and cook about 1 minute. Add chopped tomato, zucchini and eggplant. Add remaining salt, pepper and herbs. Cook, uncovered, over low heat, stirring occasionally, for 20 minutes, or until vegetables are tender and heated through. Spoon about 2 tablespoons of the filling down center of each crepe. Fold both sides up over filling. Place crepes, folded side up, in a single layer in a lightly oiled, shallow baking dish. Brush tops of crepes with melted butter. Spoon remaining ratatouille filling over tops of crepes. Bake in a preheated 400° oven for 15 minutes, or until heated through.

BUTTER COOKIES

40 cookies

1 cup butter	1 teaspoon baking soda
1½ cups sifted confectioners sugar	1 teaspoon cream of tartar
1 egg	¼ teaspoon salt
1 teaspoon vanilla extract	1 cup chopped nuts
2½ cups sifted flour	

Cream together butter and sugar until light and fluffy. Add egg and vanilla and blend well. Sift together flour, baking soda, cream of tartar and salt. Stir into butter mixture and blend thoroughly. Stir in nuts. Shape into balls the size of large marbles. Place on a baking sheet and bake in a preheated 350° oven for 10 to 12 minutes. Cool.

Helpful to know: These cookies freeze well.

HAPPY BIRTHDAY

Happy Birthday, just about anybody! Here is the kind of a party to make you happy. Have a hearty make-your-own-sandwich brunch with superb, thinly sliced beef tenderloin or glazed corned beef, both all-time favorites. Have a selection of rye breads and a good, tasty cheese bread to make delicious sandwiches. Complete the menu with pickles. And, of course, it wouldn't be a birthday without cake—Walnut Devil's Food.

Smirnoff Festive Punch
Almond Mushrooms   Lobster Barquettes
Tenderloin of Beef or Glazed Corned Beef
Assorted Rye Breads   Cheddar Cheese Bread
Grey Poupon Mustard
Green-Ripe Olives   Dill Pickles
Walnut Devil's Food Birthday Cake with Fluffy Cream-Cheese Icing
Coffee

SMIRNOFF FESTIVE PUNCH
15 to 16 drinks

1 can (46 ounces)
pineapple-grapefruit drink, chilled
1 cup cranberry juice, chilled

2 tablespoons sugar
1 cup Smirnoff Vodka

Combine juices. Add sugar and stir until well dissolved. Add vodka and pour over ice in a punch bowl.

ALMOND MUSHROOMS
1½ dozens

1 pound (about 1½ dozens)
large mushrooms
½ cup fine, dry bread crumbs
2 teaspoons lemon juice
⅛ teaspoon rosemary
⅛ teaspoon marjoram
¼ teaspoon salt

¼ cup finely chopped, blanched
almonds
1 tablespoon capers, drained
(optional)
3 tablespoons butter
3 tablespoons finely
snipped parsley

Wash mushrooms. Remove stems and reserve. Pat mushroom caps dry with paper towels. Chop mushroom stems very finely. Combine with bread crumbs, lemon juice, rosemary, marjoram, salt, almonds and capers. Spoon mixture into mushroom caps. Place in an oiled, shallow baking pan. Dot each mushroom with butter. Bake in a preheated 350° oven for 20 to 25 minutes. Sprinkle with parsley and serve immediately.

LOBSTER BARQUETTES

16 barquettes

1 package (10 ounces) pie-crust mix
1 tablespoon butter
1 can (5 ounces) lobster meat,
  finely chopped
1 tablespoon chopped onion
1 tablespoon snipped parsley

2 tablespoons brandy
2 teaspoons lemon juice
⅓ cup warm light cream
1 egg yolk
  Grated Parmesan cheese
  Buttered bread crumbs

Prepare pie-crust mix according to package directions. Roll dough out on a lightly floured board to ⅛-inch thickness. Invert 3-inch barquette molds on dough. With a sharp knife cut around molds ⅓ inch outside the edge of each mold. Fit piece of cutout pastry into each mold; press down to bottom and sides with fingertips. Trim excess pastry around rim of mold. Prick bottom all over with a fork. Fit a small piece of aluminum foil in each barquette. Fill shells with rice or beans. Bake in a preheated 375° oven for 10 minutes. Remove from oven and remove foil holding rice or beans. Return to oven and bake until bottom is lightly browned. Cool shells and remove carefully from molds. Melt butter in a skillet. Add lobster, onion and parsley. Cook gently until onion is tender but not browned. Remove from heat and stir in brandy. Sprinkle with lemon juice. Combine warm cream and egg yolk and mix well. Stir into skillet. Spoon mixture into baked barquettes. Sprinkle with Parmesan cheese and buttered crumbs. Place on broiler rack about 5 inches from source of heat and broil until tops are lightly browned.

TENDERLOIN OF BEEF

16 servings

1 whole beef tenderloin,
  about 4 to 6 pounds

1 clove garlic, halved

Rub tenderloin all over with cut side of garlic. Place on a rack in a shallow roasting pan, tucking narrow end under to make roast uniformly thick. Insert meat thermometer into center of thickest part. Roast in a preheated 450° oven for 45 to 60 minutes, or to rare (140° on the roast meat thermometer). Place meat on a carving board. At serving time, cut into very thin slices and serve with party rye bread.

GLAZED CORNED BEEF

20 servings

1 whole corned beef brisket,
  about 4 pounds
1 large onion, sliced
2 whole garlic cloves
2 bay leaves

Whole cloves
1 tablespoon Grey Poupon mustard
2 tablespoons light
  brown sugar, firmly packed

Place beef in a large dutch oven. Cover with 4 cups boiling water. Add onion, garlic and bay leaves. Bring water to a boil; reduce heat and cover. Simmer about 3½ hours, or until meat is fork-tender. Remove meat from water and place in a shallow baking pan, fat side up. Score fat and stud with cloves. Brush with mustard and sprinkle brown sugar over top. Bake in a preheated 350° oven for 15 to 20 minutes, or until well glazed on the top. Place meat on a cutting board. At serving time, cut in very thin slices and serve with party rye bread.

WALNUT DEVIL'S FOOD BIRTHDAY CAKE

1 cake

1 cup walnuts, shelled	1 teaspoon salt
Sugar	¾ cup shortening
2 cups sifted cake flour	¾ cup milk
1 tablespoon instant coffee powder	2 teaspoons vanilla extract
1¾ cups sugar	3 eggs
¾ cup cocoa	½ cup milk
1¼ teaspoons baking soda	Fluffy Cream-Cheese Icing
½ teaspoon baking powder	

Chop walnuts very finely. Generously oil sides and bottoms of two 9-inch layer cake pans. Sprinkle with sugar. Sprinkle chopped walnuts evenly over bottom of each pan. Set aside. Sift flour, coffee powder, sugar, cocoa, baking soda, baking powder and salt into a large mixing bowl. Add shortening, ¾ cup milk and vanilla. Beat 2 minutes with an electric mixer at medium speed, scraping bowl and beater often, or beat vigorously by hand about 150 strokes per minute. Add eggs and remaining ½ cup milk. Beat 2 minutes longer. Carefully spoon batter into walnut-coated pans. Bake in a preheated 350° oven for 40 to 45 minutes, or until a cake tester inserted in the center of the cake comes out clean. Let cakes stand a minute or two. Turn out onto wire racks to cool. When cake is cold, spread some of the Fluffy Cream-Cheese Icing between layers, putting the walnut-coated sides together in the center. Frost sides and top of cake with remaining icing and sprinkle additional walnuts over the top, if desired. Let cake stand until icing is set before cutting.

FLUFFY CREAM-CHEESE ICING

2 packages (3 ounces each)	⅛ teaspoon salt
cream cheese, at room temperature	¼ cup light cream
¼ cup butter, softened	4 cups sifted confectioners sugar
1 tablespoon instant coffee powder	

Beat cheese until soft. Add remaining ingredients. Beat until smooth and creamy. Spread on Walnut Devil's Food Birthday Cake.

HAPPY EASTER

Easter Day is a perfect and traditional time to have friends over and loved ones home for brunch. Plan a brunch that can be served easily after church services. Screwdrivers, with their bright orange color, belong with the sunshine of early spring. The ham can be served warm or cold; the asparagus, the first bright green spears of the year, is all ready to be set out. Then have a delicious selection of eggs and lovely hot breads on the table. What could be a nicer way to greet Easter and the beginning of spring?

Smirnoff Screwdrivers (page 17)
Orange-glazed Ham
Curried Eggs Mimosa   Asparagus Vinaigrette
Sour-Cream Biscuits
Kulich   Hot Cross Buns
Spicy Breakfast Peaches   Coffee

ORANGE-GLAZED HAM
20 servings

1 whole, fully cooked or cook-before-eating ham, semiboneless, about 8 to 10 pounds
Whole cloves (optional)

1 can (6 ounces) frozen orange juice concentrate, thawed and undiluted
¼ cup Grey Poupon mustard
¼ cup sugar

Place ham on a rack in a shallow roasting pan; bake in a preheated 325° oven for 10 minutes per pound for a fully cooked ham or 18 to 20 minutes per pound for a cook-before-eating ham. Forty-five minutes before ham is done, remove from oven. Remove rind if ham is not skinless. Make diagonal cuts ⅛ inch deep, about 1¼ inches apart, across fat side of ham. Repeat, crossing these lines to make diamonds. Insert whole cloves in each diamond, if desired. Combine orange juice, mustard and sugar. Spread over ham. Return to oven and continue baking, brushing occasionally with orange glaze.

CURRIED EGGS MIMOSA
6 servings

6 tablespoons butter
1 tablespoon curry powder
6 tablespoons flour
1 teaspoon salt

3 cups milk
½ teaspoon Tabasco sauce
9 hard-cooked eggs (page 137), shelled

Melt butter in a saucepan. Add curry powder and cook 3 to 5 minutes. Add flour and salt. Remove from heat and stir in milk. Cook over medium heat, stirring constantly, until mixture is smooth and thickened. Stir in Tabasco. Quarter hard-cooked eggs and carefully fold into cream-sauce mixture. Keep hot in a chafing dish.

ASPARAGUS VINAIGRETTE

6 servings

6 tablespoons salad oil
3 tablespoons white wine vinegar
⅛ teaspoon Tabasco sauce
½ teaspoon sugar

¼ teaspoon salt
1 small onion, thinly
   sliced and broken into rings
2 dozens cooked asparagus spears

Combine salad oil, vinegar, Tabasco, sugar and salt; beat until blended. Add onion. Pour over asparagus and let stand in the refrigerator several hours or overnight.

SOUR-CREAM BISCUITS

1 dozen

2 cups sifted flour
1 tablespoon baking powder
¼ teaspoon baking soda

1 teaspoon salt
1 cup dairy sour cream
¼ cup milk

Sift together flour, baking powder, baking soda and salt. Blend in sour cream. Stir in milk to make a soft dough. Knead gently on a lightly floured board. Pat out to ½-inch thickness. Cut in rounds with a 2-inch cutter. Place on lightly oiled baking sheet. Bake in a preheated 450° oven for 10 minutes.

KULICH

2 loaves

½ cup milk
¼ cup sugar
1 teaspoon salt
2 tablespoons butter
1 package or cake yeast,
   active dry or compressed
3 cups (about) sifted flour

1 egg
¼ cup white raisins
¼ cup chopped, blanched almonds
1 teaspoon grated lemon peel
¾ cup confectioners sugar
   Few drops vanilla extract
1 tablespoon (about) milk

Scald ½ cup milk. Stir in sugar, salt and butter. Cool to lukewarm. Measure ¼ cup warm (105°-115°) water into a bowl. Sprinkle or crumble in yeast. Stir until dissolved. Add lukewarm milk mixture. Stir in 1 cup of the flour and beat thoroughly. Beat in egg. Stir in raisins, almonds and lemon peel. Stir in about 1½ cups of the remaining flour. Sprinkle remaining flour on breadboard. Turn dough out onto flour and knead until smooth and elastic. Place into well-oiled bowl; turn dough to oil on all sides. Cover and let rise in a warm place, free from draft, until doubled in bulk, about 2 hours. Punch dough down and divide in half. Shape into 2 balls. Press each ball into an oiled 1-pound coffee can. Cover and let rise until doubled in bulk, about 1¼ hours. Bake in a preheated 350° oven for 30 to 35 minutes. Turn out of cans at once and cool. Mix confectioners sugar, vanilla and 1 tablespoon milk. Add more milk as necessary to bring icing to pouring consistency. Frost breads, letting some glaze drip down the sides.
Helpful to know: This bread freezes well. Frost bread after thawing, just before serving.

HOT CROSS BUNS
1½ dozens

¾ cup milk, scalded
½ cup shortening
⅓ cup sugar
1 teaspoon salt
1 package or cake yeast,
  active dry or compressed
1 egg, beaten

¾ cup currants
½ teaspoon mace
4 cups (about) flour
  Salad oil
1 egg white, slightly beaten
1 cup confectioners sugar
½ teaspoon vanilla extract

Combine milk, shortening, sugar and salt. Cool to lukewarm. Measure ¼ cup warm (105°-115°) water into a large warm bowl. Sprinkle or crumble in yeast. Stir until dissolved. Add milk mixture, egg, currants and mace. Stir in about 3½ cups of flour to make a stiff dough. Add more flour if needed. Place dough in an oiled bowl. Turn dough once to bring oiled side up. Cover and let rise in a warm place, free from draft, about 2 hours, or until doubled in bulk. Turn dough out onto a lightly floured surface. Knead 1 minute. Cut dough in half. Cut each half into 9 pieces. Shape each piece into a ball. Arrange balls in 2 oiled 8-inch-square pans. With oiled scissors, snip a deep cross in top of each bun. Brush with egg white. Cover and let rise in a warm place, free from draft, until doubled in bulk. Bake in a preheated 425° oven for 25 minutes, or until well browned. Cool on a wire rack. Combine confectioners sugar, 2 tablespoons hot water and vanilla. Fill in cross on each bun with sugar mixture.

SPICY BREAKFAST PEACHES
5 to 6 servings

½ cup sugar
⅓ cup red cinnamon candies
3 thin lemon slices

1 can (1 pound, 13 ounces) cling
  peach halves, drained

Combine sugar, ½ cup water, cinnamon candies and lemon slices in a saucepan. Bring to a boil and simmer 5 minutes, or until candy dissolves. Add peach halves to mixture. Simmer 5 to 6 minutes. Serve hot.

START THE YEAR RIGHT

New Year's Day is a great day for a lazy brunch. A soothing fruit punch with a pick-me-up is in order to start the year off well. A help-yourself or cook-to-order brunch will make everyone happy. The brunch table can be set with a waffle iron and a large bowl of batter. A choice of mushroomed chicken or dried beef in sour cream sauce for the main course, then a return to the table for more waffles or pancakes with a sweet topper for dessert. What could be easier or more fun? Well, it could be easier if you used frozen waffles and pancakes and a toaster!

Smirnoff Fruity Punch
Potato Waffles   Cornmeal Pancakes
Quick Mushroom Chicken   Dried Beef in Sour Cream Sauce
Maple Syrup   Cinnamon Honey Butter
Raspberries with Sour Cream
Cinnamon Cream Syrup   Golden Peach Topper
Coffee

SMIRNOFF FRUITY PUNCH
16 drinks

1 can (6 ounces) frozen
  grapefruit juice concentrate,
  undiluted
1 can (12 ounces) apricot nectar

Fresh mint leaves
½ cup sugar
2 cups Smirnoff Vodka
1 quart carbonated water

Combine grapefruit juice, apricot nectar and 2 cups water; mix well. Add a little of the liquid to a few mint leaves in a cup and crush leaves with a muddler or a spoon. Add to juice mixture. Add sugar and stir to dissolve. Pour over ice in a punch bowl. Add vodka. Slowly pour carbonated water over mixture and stir gently.

POTATO WAFFLES
8 to 10 servings

1¼ cups sifted flour
 ¼ cup instant mashed-potato granules
 2 teaspoons sugar
 2 teaspoons baking powder

½ teaspoon salt
3 eggs
⅓ cup salad oil
1½ cups milk

Sift together flour, potato granules, sugar, baking powder and salt. Beat eggs thoroughly and add salad oil and milk. Combine liquid and dry ingredients and blend thoroughly. Preheat waffle iron and pour batter into center of lower half until it spreads to about 1 inch from edges. Bake until nicely browned.

CORNMEAL PANCAKES
16 pancakes

1 cup flour
4 teaspoons baking powder
1 teaspoon salt
1 cup yellow cornmeal

1 egg
1¾ cups milk
¼ cup salad oil

Sift together flour, baking powder and salt. Stir in cornmeal. Add egg, milk and salad oil and beat until fairly smooth. Do not overbeat. Cook on hot, oiled griddle, turning once.

QUICK MUSHROOM CHICKEN

4 servings

1 envelope (1½ ounces) creamy
  mushroom-soup mix
1 cup milk

2 tablespoons diced pimiento
1½ cups diced, cooked chicken

Empty mushroom soup mix into a 1½-quart saucepan. Add milk gradually. Place over heat and stir constantly until mixture comes to a boil. Add pimiento and chicken. Heat thoroughly. Place in a chafing dish to keep warm at serving table.

DRIED BEEF IN SOUR CREAM SAUCE

4 to 6 servings

¼ pound dried beef
¼ cup butter
½ cup slivered, blanched almonds

2 tablespoons flour
2 cups dairy sour cream
12 stuffed olives, sliced

Pull the dried beef into shreds. If the beef is very salty, cover with boiling water; let stand 30 seconds and drain thoroughly. Melt butter in a saucepan. Add almonds and cook, stirring constantly, until lightly browned. Stir in flour. Remove from heat and stir in sour cream. Cook over very low heat, stirring constantly, until mixture is smooth and thickened. Bring mixture just to the boiling point, but do not boil. Stir in dried beef and olives. Keep warm in a chafing dish.

CINNAMON HONEY BUTTER

1⅓ cups

6 tablespoons butter
¼ teaspoon cinnamon

Freshly grated nutmeg
1 cup honey

Melt butter in a small saucepan. Blend in cinnamon and a dash of nutmeg. Add honey and heat just to the boiling point. Serve warm.

CINNAMON CREAM SYRUP

1⅔ cups

1 cup sugar
½ cup light corn syrup

½ teaspoon cinnamon
½ cup evaporated milk

In a small saucepan combine sugar, corn syrup, cinnamon and ¼ cup water. Bring to a boil and cook 2 minutes, stirring constantly. Remove from heat and cool for 5 minutes. Stir in the evaporated milk. Serve warm.

GOLDEN PEACH TOPPER

1⅓ cups

1 package (12 ounces) frozen peaches   1 tablespoon cornstarch
¼ cup sugar

Thaw peaches. Drain and reserve syrup. Chop peaches. In a saucepan, blend sugar and cornstarch. Stir in ¼ cup water, peaches and peach syrup. Cook, stirring constantly, until mixture comes to a boil. Continue to boil for 1 minute. Serve warm.

BRUNCH IT YOURSELF

Here are more good-for-brunch dishes—around which you can build your own, suit-yourself brunch menus.

SMIRNOFF MIDWINTER PUNCH   28 drinks

3 cups cranberry juice
2 quarts apple juice
4 sticks (2 inches each) cinnamon
1 teaspoon whole cloves

3 cups Smirnoff Vodka
Lemon slices studded
with whole cloves
Cinnamon sticks

Combine cranberry juice and apple juice. Place spices in a cheesecloth bag and tie tightly. Add spice bag to juice mixture in a saucepan and heat to boiling over medium heat. Simmer over low heat 5 minutes. Remove spice bag. Cool slightly. Add vodka. Serve hot, garnished with lemon slices and cinnamon sticks.

SMIRNOFF ORANGE-CIDER PUNCH   8 drinks

½ cup sugar
½ teaspoon cinnamon
½ teaspoon allspice
½ teaspoon nutmeg

1 cup cider
3 cups orange juice
1 cup Smirnoff Vodka

Mix sugar, cinnamon, allspice, nutmeg and cider in a large saucepan. Heat until sugar is dissolved and mixture is hot. Add orange juice and heat. Stir in vodka and serve immediately.

SMIRNOFF SPICED PUNCH   16 drinks

2 cups sugar
6 whole cloves
3 sticks (2 inches each) cinnamon
1 tablespoon diced, preserved ginger

½ cup orange juice
1½ cups grape juice
3 cups cold, strong tea
2 cups Smirnoff Vodka

Combine sugar, 2 cups water, cloves, cinnamon and preserved ginger in a saucepan. Simmer over low heat 5 minutes. Strain and cool. When cold, stir in juices, tea and vodka. Pour over ice in punch bowl.

SMIRNOFF RASPBERRY COOLER   12 drinks

1 pint raspberry sherbet
1 cup Smirnoff Vodka

1 quart dry ginger ale

Scoop sherbet into a punch bowl. Pour over vodka and ginger ale and mix gently. Serve in punch cups.

SMIRNOFF STRAWBERRY FLIP   8 drinks

2 pints strawberries,
   washed and hulled
4 eggs

6 tablespoons lemon juice
½ cup sugar
1 cup Smirnoff Vodka

Place strawberries in the container of an electric blender, cover and process at high speed to purée. Strain through cheesecloth to remove the seeds, if desired. Return to blender; add eggs, lemon juice, sugar and vodka. Cover and blend at medium speed about 15 seconds, turning off motor occasionally and stirring to redistribute mixture. Pour into tall glasses over cracked ice.

SMIRNOFF GRAPE FROTH
4 drinks

3 ounces Smirnoff Vodka
1 cup grape juice
Juice of ½ lemon

1 egg white
1 cup cracked ice

Place ingredients in container of an electric blender, cover and process at high speed for 1½ minutes. Pour into chilled cocktail glasses.

VEAL ROLL-UPS
8 servings

1 veal round steak or veal cutlets,
   cut ¼ inch thick,
   about 2 to 2½ pounds
8 thin slices boiled ham
4 slices process Swiss cheese
1 egg, slightly beaten
2 tablespoons milk

Fine, dry bread crumbs
1 can (10½ ounces) condensed
   cream of mushroom soup
2 tablespoons dry white wine
½ cup milk
Paprika

Cut veal into 8 pieces. Pound each to ⅛-inch thickness. Top each piece with a ham slice. Cut each cheese slice in 4 strips; place 2 strips each on ham slice. Roll meat around cheese. Secure with wooden picks. Mix egg and 2 tablespoons milk. Dip rolls in egg mixture, then in crumbs. Place, seam side down, in a shallow baking dish. Combine soup, wine and ½ cup milk in a saucepan. Heat. Pour around rolls. Cover baking dish with aluminum foil; bake in a preheated 350° oven for 1 hour, or until meat is tender. Uncover. Sprinkle with paprika. Bake 10 minutes, until lightly browned.

JAMBALAYA
4 to 6 servings

¼ cup butter
½ cup chopped onion
½ cup chopped green pepper
1 clove garlic, minced
1 cup uncooked rice
1 can (1 pound) tomatoes

¾ cup chicken bouillon
1 teaspoon salt
½ teaspoon Tabasco sauce
1 pound shrimp, cooked and cleaned
1½ cups diced, cooked ham

Melt butter in a large skillet. Add onion, green pepper and garlic. Cook until onion is tender but not browned. Stir in rice, tomatoes, bouillon, salt and Tabasco. Quickly bring mixture to a boil. Reduce heat, cover skillet and simmer 20 minutes. Add shrimp and ham; cover and cook 10 minutes longer, or until liquid is absorbed.

CHICKEN ZAGREB

6 servings

¼ cup butter
5 sprigs parsley, snipped
¼ pound mushrooms,
   cleaned and sliced
6 eggs, slightly beaten
¾ cup dairy sour cream

¾ cup grated Parmesan cheese
½ teaspoon Tabasco sauce
1 teaspoon salt
½ teaspoon paprika
1 cup diced, cooked chicken
6 frozen pastry shells, baked

Melt butter in a large skillet. Add parsley and mushrooms and cook over medium heat until mushrooms are just slightly cooked. Remove from heat. Combine slightly beaten eggs, sour cream, cheese, Tabasco, salt and paprika. Beat well. Add chicken to mushrooms in skillet and reheat gently. Add egg mixture and increase heat to medium high. With a spatula, lift and turn mixture until slightly thickened and piping hot. Serve in heated pastry shells.

BAKED OMELET

6 servings

6 eggs, separated
2 tablespoons cornstarch

1 teaspoon salt

Beat egg whites until stiff but not dry. Without rinsing beater, quickly beat egg yolks with cornstarch, ⅓ cup water and salt. Fold into beaten egg whites. Pour mixture into oiled glass or pottery baking dish. Bake in a preheated 350° oven for 15 minutes, or until dry on top. Serve immediately.

BRANDIED CHICKEN LIVERS

4 servings

4 tablespoons butter, divided
¼ pound sliced fresh
   mushrooms or 1 can (4
   ounces) sliced mushrooms, drained
4 scallions, chopped
1 pound chicken livers

Flour
¾ cup milk
¾ cup chicken bouillon
Salt and pepper to taste
¼ cup brandy
4 English muffins

Melt 2 tablespoons of the butter in a medium-size skillet. Add mushrooms and scallions and sauté until tender and golden brown. Remove from skillet with a slotted spoon. Cut chicken livers into bite-size pieces; pat dry with paper towels and coat well with flour. Add remaining butter to skillet and heat. Add chicken livers and brown well on all sides. Add milk and chicken bouillon and cook, stirring constantly, until mixture comes to a boil and thickens slightly. Add mushrooms, scallions and seasonings. Stir in brandy and heat thoroughly. Turn into a chafing dish and serve with split, toasted, buttered English muffins.

CRANBERRY CANADIAN BACON

10 servings

1 piece Canadian bacon,
about 4 pounds

1 can (1 pound) cranberry sauce

To remove casing on bacon, hold under cold running water, then slip off. Place bacon, fat side up, on a rack in an open roasting pan. Bake in a preheated 325° oven for 2¼ hours. Remove from oven. Melt cranberry sauce in a small saucepan over medium heat. Cover bacon with sauce. Raise oven heat to 400°. Bake bacon about 15 minutes to brown and glaze, brushing occasionally with remaining cranberry sauce. Cut in very thin slices to serve.

COTTAGE SPOON BREAD

6 servings

1¾ cups milk
½ cup cornmeal
1 teaspoon salt
1 tablespoon sugar

3 eggs, separated
3 tablespoons butter
1 cup small-curd cottage cheese

Scald milk in a medium-size saucepan. Add cornmeal and cook, stirring constantly, until thickened. Mix in salt and sugar. Blend a small amount of hot cornmeal mixture into beaten egg yolks, then return egg yolks to saucepan, mixing thoroughly. Stir in butter and cottage cheese. Beat egg whites until stiff but not dry. Fold cornmeal mixture into egg whites. Pour into an oiled 1½-quart casserole. Bake in a preheated 375° oven for 35 minutes. Serve immediately with plenty of melted butter or hot gravy.

CHICKEN LIVERS AND BEEF TIPS A LA CREME

8 servings

4 tablespoons butter, divided
½ pound mushrooms, cleaned and sliced
2 teaspoons finely chopped shallots
1 pound beef sirloin tip,
cut into 3- x ½-inch strips
1 pound chicken livers,
cut into large pieces
1 tablespoon flour

2 teaspoons paprika
1 teaspoon salt
⅛ teaspoon pepper
⅓ cup red wine vinegar
1 cup light cream
1 cup milk
2 egg yolks, lightly beaten

Melt 2 tablespoons of the butter in a skillet. Add mushrooms and cook gently 2 to 3 minutes. Remove mushrooms. Add remaining butter to skillet. Add shallots, beef and chicken livers; sprinkle with flour, paprika, salt and pepper. Cook, stirring occasionally, until browned. Add vinegar and bring just to simmering point. Cook until most of liquid is reduced. Return mushrooms to pan. Combine cream, milk and lightly beaten egg yolks. Gradually add to hot mixture. Cook a few minutes, stirring constantly, until slightly thickened and piping hot. Transfer mixture to heated chafing dish for serving. Serve over hot buttered noodles, if desired.

SHRIMP VOL-AU-VENT

6 servings

1 can (6 ounces)
broiled-in-butter mushroom crowns
⅓ cup butter
2 teaspoons minced onion
⅓ cup flour
1 teaspoon salt
Few grains pepper

⅛ teaspoon nutmeg
1 cup milk
1 cup light cream
1 egg yolk
2 pounds shrimp, cooked and cleaned
½ cup dry sherry
6 frozen patty shells, baked

Drain mushrooms, reserving liquid. Melt butter in a saucepan. Add minced onion and cook about 3 minutes over low heat until soft but not browned. Blend in flour, salt, pepper and nutmeg. Add milk, cream and liquid from mushrooms. Cook over medium heat, stirring constantly, until mixture is smooth and thickened. Beat egg yolk slightly. Add a little of the hot mixture to egg, blend well and return egg to saucepan. Mix well. Cook over low heat, stirring constantly, about 3 minutes. Combine shrimp, mushrooms and sherry in a saucepan. Heat over low heat about 5 minutes. Add shrimp mixture to hot sauce and stir enough to just blend. Serve mixture in hot patty shells.

FRENCH POTTED CHEESE

1 quart

1½ pounds Cheddar cheese, grated
1 cup dairy sour cream
1¼ teaspoons salt
⅛ teaspoon cayenne

¼ teaspoon mace
5 tablespoons (about) dry white wine
½ cup melted butter

Place all ingredients in electric blender. Cover and blend until very smooth and creamy, adding a little more wine if necessary. Pack mixture into small molds or jars. Cover tightly and store in refrigerator 24 hours before using. Turn out of molds and place on serving platter. Serve with slices of fruit, if desired.

PECAN OMELET

2 servings

½ pound medium-size mushrooms,
washed and trimmed
2 tablespoons butter
2 cups cooked peas
4 eggs, well beaten

Dash of salt
Dash of pepper
¼ cup heavy cream
3 tablespoons butter
⅓ cup ground pecans

Sauté mushrooms in 2 tablespoons butter until tender. Heat peas. Season eggs in bowl with salt and pepper; stir in cream. Melt 3 tablespoons butter in skillet; add egg mixture. Sprinkle with pecans. Cook over low heat, lifting omelet from time to time to prevent sticking. Turn omelet onto warm platter, folded in half. Cover with mushrooms and circle with peas. Serve at once.

BONUS: ALL ABOUT WONDER CAKES

A plain, unfrosted cake, not too sweet, is just the right thing to serve when you want something for a brunch dessert other than fruit or a sweet bread of some sort. These Wonder Pound Cakes have just about everything going for them: They are easy to make (a box of cake mix is the basis for each of them, plus a touch of inventiveness); they keep beautifully, so you may make them well in advance of the time you'll serve them. They need no frosting—a dusting of confectioners sugar finishes them handsomely; you may use a glaze if you like, but even that seems a bit like lily-gilding. Store these cakes tightly covered; cut in thin slices to serve. Once you've got the hang of it, try inventing new Wonder Cake combinations.

General directions: Turn all ingredients into the large bowl of an electric mixer. Using a rubber spatula to push ingredients into mixer blades, mix at low speed until ingredients are well blended. Beat at medium speed 4 minutes. Bake in an oiled 10-inch tube pan (or bundt pan) in a preheated 350° oven for 45 to 55 minutes, or until the cake tests done with a toothpick or cake tester. Each cake makes about 16 servings.

Lucia Wonder Cake

1 package yellow-cake mix
4 eggs
½ cup cooking oil
1 cup water
1 package (3½ ounces) vanilla
instant-pudding mix

1 teaspoon ground cardamom
¾ cup blanched almonds,
finely chopped

Mix all ingredients except almonds as above. Stir in almonds. Bake according to general directions above.

Lemon Wonder Cake

1 package yellow-cake mix
4 eggs
½ cup cooking oil
⅞ cup water

2 tablespoons lemon juice
1 package (3½ ounces) lemon
instant-pudding mix
2 teaspoons grated lemon peel

Mix and bake according to general directions given above.

57

Mocha Wonder Cake

1 package chocolate *or* devil's food cake mix
4 eggs
½ cup cooking oil
1 cup water

1 package (3½ ounces) chocolate instant-pudding mix
2 tablespoons instant coffee powder
1 teaspoon vanilla extract

Mix and bake according to general directions given above.

Virginia Wonder Cake

1 package yellow-cake mix
4 eggs
½ cup cooking oil
1 cup water

1 package (3½ ounces) vanilla instant-pudding mix
1½ teaspoons ground mace

Mix and bake according to general directions given above.

Orange-Plus Wonder Cake

1 package white-cake mix
4 eggs
½ cup cooking oil
1 cup orange juice

1 package (3½ ounces) vanilla instant-pudding mix
1 tablespoon grated orange peel
½ teaspoon ground nutmeg

Mix and bake according to directions given above.

Wine-Walnut Wonder Cake

1 package white-cake mix
4 eggs
½ cup cooking oil
½ cup water

½ cup dry sherry
1 package (3½ ounces) vanilla instant-pudding mix
¾ cup chopped walnuts

Mix all ingredients except nuts as above. Stir in nuts by hand. Bake according to general directions given above.

Sugar-and-Spice Wonder Cake

2 tablespoons butter
¼ cup sugar
2 teaspoons cinnamon, divided
1 cup chopped toasted almonds, divided

1 package white-cake mix
4 eggs
½ cup cooking oil
1 package (3½ ounces) vanilla instant-pudding mix

Using the butter, liberally oil a 10-inch tube pan. Combine sugar and 1 teaspoon cinnamon and sprinkle carefully over the bottom and sides of the pan. Sprinkle the bottom of the pan with ¼ cup almonds. Mix remaining ingredients, except almonds, as above. Stir in almonds by hand. Spoon batter carefully into pan, disturbing the sugar mixture and almonds as little as possible. Bake according to general directions above.

BEFORE THE GAME

ALL ON A SUMMER'S DAY

It's the "in" thing to watch football, baseball, basketball and hockey on TV in the comfort of your own home in the company of good friends. Today he's going to be watching the baseball game, right? And you're not. So instead of doing the mending, as your conscience tells you, invite company for brunch—then he'll have companions for his game-watching and you can neatly avoid the mending by gabbing with the girls.

Smirnoff Sangarees
Guacamole   Corn Chips
Cold Poached Salmon with Dill Sauce
Cucumber Boats   Artichoke Devils
Hot Croissants   Lemon Marmalade   Hot Brioche
Fresh Peaches   Maids of Honor
Iced Tea

SMIRNOFF SANGAREE
1 drink

½ teaspoon confectioners sugar

2 ounces Smirnoff Vodka

Carbonated water

1 tablespoon Harvey's Gold Cap Port

Dissolve sugar in 1 teaspoon water in an 8-ounce glass. Add vodka and 2 cubes of ice. Fill with carbonated water; stir. Float port on top of drink.

GUACAMOLE
8 servings

2 ripe avocados, peeled and pitted

2 teaspoons onion juice

4 teaspoons lime juice

½ teaspoon coriander

1 tomato, peeled, seeded and finely chopped

Salt to taste

Cut avocados in chunks; place in blender container. Add remaining ingredients. Cover and process at medium speed until well blended. Chill until ready to serve.

COLD POACHED SALMON WITH DILL SAUCE
8 servings

1 piece of salmon, about 5 pounds

2 cups dry white wine

1 small onion, peeled and halved

2 tablespoons lemon juice

Salt and white pepper to taste

Measure the salmon at its highest point. Multiply the number of inches by 10—the result is the number of minutes of cooking time needed. (Example: If a salmon measures 4 inches, the cooking time will be 40 minutes.) Combine wine, onion, lemon juice, salt and pepper in a deep kettle and add enough water to cover salmon. Bring to a boil. Wrap salmon in cheesecloth, leaving enough material at the top to use for a handle. When wine-water mixture boils, lower salmon gently into it; bring water back to simmering point and simmer salmon required number of minutes. Using cheesecloth handle, remove from cooking liquid. Drain well; refrigerate. Just before serving, remove cheesecloth, transfer to serving plate and remove skin if desired. Serve salmon lifted neatly off the bones.

DILL SAUCE
8 servings

2 cups dairy sour cream
2 tablespoons lemon juice

¼ cup snipped fresh dillweed
Salt and white pepper to taste

Mix all ingredients. Chill.
Helpful to know: If you can't find fresh dill, packaged dillweed from your grocer's spice shelf will do fine.

CUCUMBER BOATS
8 servings

4 small cucumbers
2 tablespoons grated onion
¼ cup finely chopped celery
2 tablespoons snipped parsley
8 large mushrooms, chopped

4 tablespoons finely diced
Swiss cheese
French Dressing (page 87)
Salt and pepper to taste

Peel cucumbers and cut in half lengthwise. With a spoon, scoop out the seeds and the membrane around them, leaving small "boats." Combine onion, celery, parsley, mushrooms and cheese with just enough French Dressing to coat the ingredients. Season to taste. Mound into cucumber shells and refrigerate until ready to serve.

ARTICHOKE DEVILS
8 servings

8 hard-cooked eggs (page 137)
1½ to 2 tablespoons
whipped sweet butter
1 teaspoon onion juice
Salt and white pepper to taste
1 package (10½ ounces) frozen
artichoke hearts

¼ cup wine vinegar
¼ cup olive oil
1 teaspoon salt
¼ teaspoon freshly ground
black pepper
Paprika

As soon as eggs are cool enough to handle, shell them, cut in halves lengthwise, and turn yolks into a small bowl. With a fork, mash thoroughly. Add enough butter to make a thick paste, remembering that the paste will thicken after the eggs are refrigerated. Add onion juice and salt and pepper to taste. Fill whites; cover and refrigerate. Cook artichoke hearts according to package directions. Cut each in half lengthwise. Combine vinegar, oil, salt and pepper and marinate artichoke pieces in this liquid overnight. To serve, drain artichokes and place one on the yolk of each deviled egg; sprinkle with paprika.

MAIDS OF HONOR
12 servings

Pastry for one 9-inch pie crust
2 eggs
¼ cup sugar
2 teaspoons flour
⅛ teaspoon salt
1½ cups milk
1 teaspoon vanilla extract
½ cup ground, toasted almonds

Roll out pastry on a lightly floured pastry cloth or board to a thickness of ⅛ inch. Cut into 12 circles 4 inches in diameter. (Circles may be made by tracing with a paring knife the outside of a 4-inch teacup or by using a paper pattern cut 4 inches in diameter.) Fit pastry circles into 2½-inch muffin cups; set aside. Slightly beat eggs in a mixing bowl. Mix together sugar, flour and salt; stir into eggs. Add milk and vanilla; mix thoroughly. Stir in almonds. Pour into pastry cups. Bake in a preheated 450° oven for 10 minutes; reduce oven temperature to 325° and bake 20 minutes longer, or until tip of knife inserted in the center of the custard comes out clean. Remove pan from oven and let cool on a wire rack 10 minutes.

HINT OF AUTUMN

The days are getting hazy. Here and there a leaf is beginning to turn, and at night there's a definite chill in the air. But you really know it's autumn because next Saturday the first pro football game will be on TV—not a preseason game, but the first honest-to-goodness one. You can't fight it; instead, you give in with good grace and decide to welcome the season with a brunch party. Sweet corn is still around, so you'll make a corn pudding. The coffee cake—a very special one—has been mellowing for several days, growing better by the minute.

Smirnoff Screwdrivers
(page 17)
Pickled Mushrooms   Wheat Thins
Sweet-Corn Pudding   Little Pork Sausages
Cheddar Scrambled Eggs
Spicy Honey Bread   Persimmon Halves
Coffee

PICKLED MUSHROOMS

8 servings

1 large onion, minced
1 clove garlic, minced
2 cups dry white wine
½ cup cider vinegar
2 bay leaves
½ teaspoon thyme

½ teaspoon pepper
½ teaspoon salt
½ cup olive oil
1½ pounds button mushrooms
Snipped chives

Combine onion, garlic, wine, vinegar, bay leaves, thyme, pepper and salt in a saucepan. Bring to a boil and simmer 5 minutes. Add oil. Wash mushrooms and pat dry. Remove stems and reserve for another use; put caps in wine-vinegar mixture; simmer until mushrooms are barely tender, 8 to 10 minutes. Refrigerate until ready to serve. Sprinkle with chives; serve with food picks for spearing.

SWEET-CORN PUDDING

8 servings

3 cups (about 8 ears) fresh corn, scraped from the cob
2 tablespoons flour
1½ teaspoons sugar

1 cup light cream
Salt and white pepper to taste
Butter

Score the ears of corn by running a knife lengthwise through the rows of kernels. With the dull edge of the knife, scrape corn from the cobs, removing all milky pulp. Mix flour and sugar with corn. Stir in cream gradually. Season lightly with salt and pepper. Generously oil a 9-inch-square baking dish. Pour in corn mixture. Dot the top with butter. Bake in a preheated 325° oven for 1 hour, or until lightly browned and set.

SPICY HONEY BREAD

2 loaves

⅔ cup honey
1 cup sugar
4 cups finely milled rye flour
1 teaspoon baking soda
4 teaspoons baking powder
1½ tablespoons cinnamon

1 teaspoon ground cloves
1 teaspoon ground allspice
¼ teaspoon ground cardamom
¾ cup shredded, blanched almonds
2 tablespoons grated orange peel
¾ cup finely chopped citron

In the top of a double boiler heat honey, 1½ cups water and sugar until small bubbles appear. Mix flour, baking soda, baking powder and spices. Beat in the honey mixture. Beat 10 minutes with electric mixer at medium speed. Beat in nuts, peel and citron. Pour mixture into two oiled 8- x 4½-inch loaf pans. Place a pan of water on lowest shelf of oven. Bake bread on top shelf in preheated 350° oven for about 1 hour.

Helpful to know: Like good wine, this ages gracefully. Will keep 2 weeks, and should be aged at least 3 days in plastic or tin before serving.

THE SNOW BEGINS TO FLY

There's a game to watch on TV this afternoon, but first everybody will want a hearty brunch—just the sight of snow makes people ravenous, and if you all go out for a walk in it before eating, appetites will be boundless. While your guests (you, too) warm up with Smirnoff Hawkshots and stave off starvation with crackers and Liptauer, the chops and brussels sprouts finish baking. With forethought, you made the corn bread before the guests arrived, and now it needs only a brief warming. Yesterday you stirred a cup of chopped walnuts into a jar of cranberry-orange relish, so that's ready too. And you made the cake yesterday. Relax, enjoy!

Smirnoff Hawkshots
Assorted Crackers   Liptauer Cheese
Stuffed Pork Chops   Brussels Sprouts with Chestnuts
Cranberry-Orange-Walnut Relish
Corn-Bread Squares   Maple Butter
Mahogany Cake with Mocha Frosting
Coffee

SMIRNOFF HAWKSHOT
1 drink

2 ounces Smirnoff 100-proof Vodka   1 beef-bouillon cube
1 lemon quarter

Place vodka in a mug. Squeeze in lemon juice and discard pulp. Add bouillon cube. Fill mug with very hot water, stirring.

LIPTAUER CHEESE
12 servings

1 package (8 ounces)
   cream cheese, at room temperature
⅓ cup butter, softened
2 teaspoons chopped capers

4 anchovy fillets, finely chopped
2 shallots, minced
½ teaspoon caraway seed (optional)
¾ teaspoon salt

Mix ingredients thoroughly and form into a roll; wrap in plastic wrap or aluminum foil. Let mellow in the refrigerator at least overnight.

STUFFED PORK CHOPS
8 servings

8 loin pork chops, cut 1 inch thick
1 cup chopped onion
1 cup chopped celery
1 package (7 ounces)
   herb-seasoned bread-cube stuffing

Salt and pepper to taste
½ teaspoon sage
¼ teaspoon thyme
¼ cup snipped parsley

Trim some of the fat from the chops. Fry this fat gently in a skillet; remove solid particles and brown the chops lightly in the liquid fat. Remove chops from skillet; place onion and celery in skillet and cook until tender but not browned. Prepare stuffing according to package directions. Combine with vegetables and seasonings. Using two long skewers, form chops into a loaf in a baking pan, bone side down, leaving about an inch between each two chops. Place stuffing between chops—if any remains, spoon it into the pan. Bake in a preheated 325° oven for 1 hour, or until tender.

BRUSSELS SPROUTS WITH CHESTNUTS   8 servings

3 cups cooked brussels sprouts	Beef bouillon
¾ pound cooked chestnuts	Fine, dry bread crumbs
Salt and pepper to taste	Butter
Butter	Paprika

Oil a 2-quart casserole. Fill with alternate layers of sprouts and chestnuts, seasoning each layer lightly with salt and pepper and dotting each layer with butter. Moisten lightly with bouillon. Sprinkle heavily with bread crumbs. Dot with butter; sprinkle with paprika. Bake in a preheated 350° oven for 30 minutes.

CORN-BREAD SQUARES   16 squares

½ cup sifted flour	1½ cups yellow cornmeal
2½ teaspoons baking powder	1 egg, beaten
1½ tablespoons sugar	3 tablespoons melted butter
¼ teaspoon salt	¾ cup milk

Sift together flour, baking powder, sugar and salt. Mix in cornmeal. Add egg to melted butter and milk. Pour liquid over dry ingredients and mix quickly—do not beat. Bake in a hot, buttered 9- x 9-inch pan in a preheated 425° oven for about 25 minutes. Cut into squares.

MAPLE BUTTER   16 servings

¾ cup butter, softened	½ teaspoon maple flavoring
¼ cup light brown sugar, firmly packed	

Beat ingredients together until well blended. Refrigerate until ready to serve.

MAHOGANY CAKE   10 to 12 servings

1½ cups butter, softened	1½ cups sifted flour
1¼ cups sugar	½ teaspoon salt
3 eggs	1 teaspoon baking powder
2 squares (1 ounce each) unsweetened chocolate, cut up	1 teaspoon baking soda
	2 teaspoons vanilla extract
1 cup very strong, hot coffee	Mocha Frosting

64

Oil two 8-inch layer-cake pans. Cream the butter and sugar together until light and fluffy. Add the eggs, 1 at a time, beating after each addition. Blend the chocolate and the hot coffee, stirring until the chocolate is melted. Sift the dry ingredients together, and add to the butter mixture, alternating with the coffee-chocolate mixture. Add the vanilla. Spread in the prepared pans. Bake in a preheated 350° oven for about 30 minutes, or until the cake springs back when touched lightly in the center and has begun to shrink from the sides of the pans. Turn out on wire racks and cool. Frost bottom layer with Mocha Frosting, put second layer on top and frost.

MOCHA FROSTING

1¼ cups (about) confectioners sugar
½ cup unsweetened cocoa
2 tablespoons butter
½ teaspoon cinnamon

1 teaspoon instant coffee powder
Pinch of salt
2 tablespoons light cream

Place all ingredients in a saucepan and cook, stirring, over low heat for 5 or 6 minutes. If not thick enough to spread, add a little more sugar. Beat well and spread on a cold cake.

DOING SOMETHING ABOUT IT

The weather, that is. When there's baseball to watch on a scorching summer's day, make the game twice as welcome by preceding it with a memorable brunch, one that can be prepared ahead of time. Set the table indoors if the heat outside is too much to bear or on the patio—or even under a tree—if there is the possibility of a breeze. If game time comes too soon for the brunchers, serve dessert and coffee to them during the seventh-inning stretch.

Smirnoff and Tonics
Smoked Salmon Spread   Crisp Crackers
Cold Senegalese Soup
Salade Niçoise   Mustard Deviled Eggs
Thin Slices of Cold Baked Ham
Toasted French Bread   Sweet Butter
Cold Strawberry Soufflé   Madeleines
Coffee

SMIRNOFF AND TONIC

1 drink

2 ounces Smirnoff Vodka
Quinine water

Wedge of fresh lime

Put vodka and several cubes of ice into a 12-ounce glass. Fill with quinine water. Squeeze lime wedge over drink and drop into glass. Stir and serve.

SMOKED SALMON SPREAD

16 servings

1 package (8 ounces)
   cream cheese, at room temperature
½ cup finely diced, smoked salmon

1 teaspoon freshly ground
   black pepper
2 tablespoons lemon juice

Combine ingredients, blending thoroughly with a fork until of a good spreading consistency.

COLD SENEGALESE SOUP

8 servings

3 tablespoons butter
2 to 3 teaspoons curry powder
2 tablespoons flour
4 cups chicken broth

3 egg yolks
1 cup light cream
   Snipped chives

Melt butter and stir in curry powder. Add the flour, stirring constantly. Slowly stir in chicken broth. Bring to a boil. Reduce heat. Beat together egg yolks and cream. Stir slowly into soup. Cook, stirring, over low heat until thickened slightly. Do not boil. Cool, then chill. Garnish with chives.

SALADE NIÇOISE

12 servings

3 cups cooked green beans, chilled
6 tomatoes, peeled and quartered
   French Dressing (page 87)
½ cup dry white wine
3 cups cooked, peeled and
   sliced new potatoes

1 can (7 ounces) tuna fish, drained
2 tablespoons drained capers
   Salad greens
½ cup small, pitted ripe olives
12 anchovy fillets

Combine green beans and tomatoes; marinate in French Dressing in the refrigerator at least 3 hours. Heat the wine and pour over potato slices. Let stand at room temperature for 1 hour. Place tuna fish in the center of a serving platter. Mound potatoes at one side and sprinkle with capers. Surround with salad greens. Drain beans and tomatoes and place on salad greens in separate mounds. Garnish with olives and anchovy fillets.

MUSTARD DEVILED EGGS

12 servings

12 hard-cooked eggs (page 137)
   Butter, softened
   Grey Poupon mustard

Salt and white pepper to taste
24 small sprigs of parsley

As soon as eggs are cool enough to handle, shell them, cut into halves lengthwise, and turn yolks into a bowl. With a fork, mash thoroughly. Stir in enough soft butter to make a smooth paste. (Remember that the paste will become stiffer when the eggs are chilled.) Stir in mustard to taste. Add salt (taste—it may not be necessary) and a little white pepper. Fill egg whites. Top each egg half with a sprig of parsley.

COLD STRAWBERRY SOUFFLE

12 servings

1 quart strawberries,
  washed and hulled
2½ cups sugar, divided
2 envelopes unflavored gelatin

8 eggs, separated
¼ teaspoon salt
2 cups heavy cream, whipped

Fold a long strip of waxed paper or aluminum foil so that it is about 4 inches wide and long enough to extend around the outside of a 3-quart soufflé dish. Lightly brush one side of the strip with oil. Fasten the strip, oiled side in, around top of soufflé dish. It can be tied with string or clipped together with paper clips. Put berries in container of a blender, cover and purée. Pour berries into a 1-quart measure. There should be about 2⅔ cups purée. Stir 1 cup sugar into the berries. Remove ½ cup of the purée. Sprinkle gelatin over top and let stand to soften. Combine egg yolks with 1 cup sugar in top of double boiler. Cook over boiling water, stirring until mixture is thickened. Add gelatin mixture and stir until gelatin is dissolved. Cool. Blend in remaining purée. Beat egg whites and salt until foamy. Gradually add ½ cup sugar and continue beating until mixture is shiny and forms stiff peaks. Fold in whipped cream. Gently fold in strawberry mixture. Turn mixture into prepared soufflé dish. Chill until firm. Remove collar and serve.

MADELEINES

15 little cakes

¾ cup butter
2 eggs
1 cup sugar

1 cup sifted cake flour
1 tablespoon Don Q White Rum
2 teaspoons grated lemon peel

Melt butter and allow to cool. In the top of a double boiler heat together the eggs and sugar until lukewarm, stirring constantly. Remove from heat and beat until thickened, light and pale, beating as much air into the mixture as possible. Sift flour and add gradually. Add the melted butter, rum and lemon peel. Spoon into madeleine shells or small muffin tins. Bake in a preheated 450° oven for about 15 minutes.

BRUNCH IT YOURSELF

Here are more good-for-brunch dishes—around which you can build your own, suit-yourself brunch menus.

SMIRNOFF AND PORT
1 drink

¼ ounce Harvey's Gold Cap Port   1 thin lime slice
2½ ounces Smirnoff Vodka

In a cocktail shaker, stir port and vodka with 1 ice cube. Pour into a chilled cocktail glass and float lime slice.

SMIRNOFF CURAÇAO SCREWDRIVER
1 drink

1½ ounces Smirnoff Vodka   Chilled orange juice
½ ounce Arrow Curaçao

Place 2 ice cubes in an 8-ounce glass. Add vodka, Curaçao and orange juice to fill glass. Stir.

SMIRNOFF BURNISHED BRASS
1 drink

¾ ounce Harvey's Amontillado Sherry   1½ ounces Smirnoff Vodka

Shake together with cracked ice. Strain into a chilled cocktail glass.

SMIRNOFF DILL MARY
1 drink

½ teaspoon dried dillweed   1 drop Tabasco sauce
1½ ounces Smirnoff Vodka   ⅛ teaspoon salt
3 ounces tomato juice   Light grinding of pepper

Rub dill between fingers to powder and drop into bar glass or cup. Pour in vodka and tomato juice. Let stand for 10 minutes. Add Tabasco and salt. Stir. Strain through fine mesh strainer over ice cubes into an 8-ounce glass. Stir until thoroughly chilled. Grind a light sprinkle of black pepper over top.

ISLAND FIGS
4 servings

2 large oranges, peeled and sliced   1 teaspoon lemon juice
8 large figs, peeled and sliced   ¼ cup flaked coconut
¼ to ⅓ cup sugar

Place orange slices in a serving bowl. Cover with figs and sprinkle with sugar, lemon juice and coconut. Chill.

EGGS IN MUSHROOM CAPS

8 servings

16 large (2½ to 3½ inches in
   diameter each) mushrooms
1 cup butter
16 eggs

Salt to taste
1 cup shredded Gruyère
   or Swiss cheese
Toast points

Wash mushrooms and pat dry. Carefully remove stem from each mushroom and hollow cap slightly with a small spoon. (Save scraps and stems for other uses.) In a large skillet, melt the butter and brown the mushrooms lightly on all sides, basting them with the butter occasionally. Keep the mushrooms warm in a low oven. Poach eggs as directed on page 138. Drain eggs and place 1 in each mushroom cap; trim white if necessary to make fit. Baste with a little of the cooking butter, sprinkle with salt, and top with shredded cheese. Place on broiler rack 4 inches from source of heat and broil until cheese bubbles. Serve with toast points.

EGGS WITH OYSTERS AND BACON

4 servings

1 jar (12 ounces) small
   oysters, drained
½ teaspoon salt
1 egg
1 cup minced filberts
½ cup flour

6 slices raw bacon, chopped
8 eggs
1 teaspoon Worcestershire sauce
2 dashes Tabasco sauce
2 tablespoons brandy
1 tablespoon snipped chives

Sprinkle oysters with salt. Beat 1 egg with 1 tablespoon water and add oysters. In a bag combine nuts and flour; lift oysters with a fork, a few at a time, from egg and drop into bag. Shake to coat well. Arrange oysters in a single layer on a small tray; sprinkle any remaining nut mixture over them. Cover lightly and chill at least 30 minutes. In a large skillet, cook the bacon over medium-high heat until crisp. Remove bacon and reserve. To drippings, add the oysters and brown on each side; do not crowd. (If necessary, remove a few of the cooked oysters from the pan to make room for the remaining ones.) While oysters are cooking, break 8 eggs into a bowl and beat with Worcestershire and Tabasco. Add brandy to oysters and ignite; pour the eggs into pan around the oysters. Reduce heat and cook until eggs are set. Slide a wide spatula under oysters to let egg flow to bottom of pan. Sprinkle with snipped chives and cooked bacon. Serve directly from skillet.

CORN DOLLARS

4 servings

4 ears fresh corn, or 1 can
   (12 ounces) whole-kernel corn,
   drained and coarsely chopped
4 eggs

¼ cup light cream or evaporated milk
½ teaspoon salt
½ cup wheat germ

Score the ears of fresh corn by running a knife lengthwise through the rows of kernels. With the dull edge of the knife, scrape the corn from the cobs, removing all the milky pulp from each ear. Put into a mixing bowl. Add eggs, cream, salt and wheat germ; beat thoroughly until well blended. The batter should be quite thin. If it is too thin, add more wheat germ. Drop by small spoonfuls onto a moderately hot, well-oiled griddle. Bake slowly until browned; turn and brown the other side. Serve hot from the griddle.

ORANGE WAFFLES

8 servings

8 eggs, separated
1⅓ cups sugar
½ cup milk
⅓ cup melted butter, cooled

4 teaspoons grated orange peel
2 cups sifted flour
1 teaspoon salt
¼ cup sugar

Beat egg yolks with the 1⅓ cups sugar until thick and pale yellow; beat in the milk, butter and orange peel. Sift flour again with the salt. Beat egg whites until soft peaks form; gradually beat in the ¼ cup sugar until mixture is glossy. Fold egg yolk mixture and flour into beaten egg whites. Spoon batter into preheated waffle iron and bake until lightly browned.

BUTTERSCOTCH SAUCE FOR WAFFLES

1⅔ cups

2 cups dark brown sugar, firmly packed
¼ cup butter
½ cup evaporated milk

Dash of salt
1 teaspoon vanilla extract

In the top of a double boiler, combine the brown sugar, butter, evaporated milk and salt. Cook over boiling water, stirring frequently, for about 15 minutes. Stir in the vanilla. Keep warm over hot water until serving time. If necessary, thin the sauce with additional evaporated milk.

CHICKEN SHORTCAKE

6 servings

6 large slices of cooked
  chicken or turkey
6 tablespoons butter, divided
¼ cup flour
Few grains nutmeg

1 cup light cream
1 cup chicken broth
½ cup coarsely chopped, salted peanuts
Salt to taste
Hot Corn-Bread Squares (page 64)

Sauté the chicken slices in 3 tablespoons of the butter. Remove chicken and keep it warm while sauce is being prepared. Add 3 tablespoons butter to pan and blend in flour and nutmeg. Gradually stir in the cream and broth. Cook, stirring constantly, until sauce is thick and smooth. Add peanuts and salt. Split corn-bread squares in half. Arrange the chicken slices over bottom halves of corn bread. Replace top halves and serve with the hot peanut gravy.

THE TRY-AND-TASTE BRUNCH

SALAD DAYS

The order of the day: something new and something different. Instead of the tried-and-true one-main-dish brunch, you are going to have a smorgasbord of similar dishes and everyone can try and taste a little of each one. Because the year is young and green, put together a bevy of salads as savory as they are handsome. All the salads in this menu can be prepared in advance—the day ahead, if you like.

Smirnoff Salty Dogs (page 28)
Cosmopolitan Lobster Salad   Perfect Chicken Salad
Beef Salad   Peach-Almond Soufflé Salad
Celery Rémoulade
Platter of Assorted Pickles and Olives
Bran Toaster Cakes   Corn Toaster Cakes
Ambrosia   Dundee Cake
Coffee

COSMOPOLITAN LOBSTER SALAD
4 servings

1½ cups cubed, cooked lobster meat
½ cup chopped celery
2 hard-cooked eggs (page 137), shelled and chopped
2 tablespoons chili sauce
1 cup mayonnaise
1 tablespoon lemon juice
Salt and pepper to taste
Lettuce leaves
6 stuffed olives, sliced

Combine lobster, celery and eggs. Add chili sauce to mayonnaise. Stir in lemon juice. Season, pour over salad and toss lightly. Line a serving bowl with lettuce leaves. Place salad in bowl and garnish with olives.

PERFECT CHICKEN SALAD
4 servings

2½ cups bite-size pieces of cold, cooked chicken
Salt and white pepper to taste
Blender Lemon Mayonnaise
Spears of Belgian endive
3 tablespoons drained capers

Place chicken in a bowl. Season lightly with salt and pepper. Add enough lemon mayonnaise to coat the pieces of chicken. Line a shallow serving bowl with spears of endive, points up. Mound chicken salad in the center. Sprinkle with capers.

73

BLENDER LEMON MAYONNAISE

1½ cups

1 egg
2 tablespoons lemon juice
1 strip lemon peel

½ teaspoon dry mustard
1 teaspoon salt
1 cup salad oil, divided

Place egg and lemon juice in blender container. Using a vegetable peeler, cut off a strip of lemon peel; add to blender container along with mustard, salt and ½ cup oil. Cover; process at medium speed a few seconds. Without turning off blender, remove center cover and add remaining oil in a thin stream. Serve at once or refrigerate.

BEEF SALAD

4 servings

1¼ cups diced, cold, cooked beef
1 small onion, thinly sliced
1¼ cups diced, cold, cooked potatoes
Boston lettuce leaves
2 teaspoons snipped parsley
1 teaspoon anchovy paste

2 tablespoons red wine vinegar
4 tablespoons salad oil
Salt and black pepper to taste
1 hard-cooked egg (page 137), shelled and sieved

Mix meat, onion and potatoes. Line serving bowl with lettuce leaves; place meat mixture in center. Combine remaining ingredients except egg and pour over. Garnish with egg.

PEACH-ALMOND SOUFFLE SALAD

4 servings

1 package (3 ounces) orange-flavored gelatin
2 tablespoons lemon juice
½ cup mayonnaise
¼ teaspoon salt

1½ cups diced, canned cling peaches, well drained
1 package (3 ounces) cream cheese, at room temperature
¼ cup toasted, slivered almonds

Pour 1 cup hot water over gelatin in large bowl of electric mixer. Stir until gelatin is dissolved. Add ½ cup cold water, lemon juice, mayonnaise and salt. Beat at medium speed until well blended. Pour into freezing tray and chill in freezer or refrigerator until firm, 20 to 25 minutes. Chill mixer bowl. Meanwhile combine peaches, cheese and almonds. Turn gelatin into chilled bowl. Beat at high speed until thick and fluffy. Fold in peach mixture. Pour into a 1-quart mold. Chill until firm. Unmold on chilled plate.

CELERY REMOULADE

4 servings

2 bunches celery hearts
2 tablespoons lemon juice
2 teaspoons salt
¼ cup Grey Poupon mustard
⅓ cup olive oil
2 to 3 tablespoons white wine vinegar

½ teaspoon salt
⅓ teaspoon white pepper
Salad greens
3 tablespoons finely snipped parsley
2 teaspoons finely snipped chives

Wash and dry celery. Cut into small julienne strips. Place in a bowl, add lemon juice and 2 teaspoons salt. Mix well and let stand at room temperature 1 hour. To make dressing, warm large electric mixer bowl by rinsing with hot water; dry. Place mustard in bowl. Beating at low-medium speed, add 3 tablespoons boiling water, a few drops at a time. Continuing to beat, add the oil, a few drops at a time. Add 2 tablespoons vinegar, ½ teaspoon salt and the pepper. Taste and add more vinegar and seasonings if necessary. Add dressing to celery and mix gently. Refrigerate, covered, overnight. Line a serving bowl with greens and mound celery in bowl. Sprinkle with parsley and chives.

AMBROSIA
4 servings

2 large, seedless oranges
3 ripe bananas
⅓ cup confectioners sugar

1½ cups shredded coconut
Mint leaves, chopped

Peel and section oranges. Peel and slice bananas. Mix sugar and coconut. Layer fruit and coconut mixture in a serving bowl. Chill. Sprinkle with mint.

DUNDEE CAKE
10 servings

¾ cup butter, softened
⅔ cup sugar
3 eggs
2 cups sifted flour
1 teaspoon baking powder
½ teaspoon salt

1 cup currants
¾ cup chopped, pitted dates
¾ cup white raisins
½ cup chopped, mixed citrus peel
3 tablespoons split blanched almonds

Cream butter and sugar until light and fluffy. Add eggs, 1 at a time, beating well after each addition. Reserve 2 tablespoons flour; sift remaining flour with baking powder and salt. Add flour—baking-powder mixture to butter, blending thoroughly. Mix the reserved flour with the fruits until they are well coated. Stir in fruit and mixed peel. Spoon into an oiled 8-inch-square cake pan. Bake in preheated 350° oven for 30 minutes. Arrange almonds attractively on top. Reduce heat to 325° and bake for 30 minutes longer, or until cake tests done.

TAKE IT EASY

The simplest and—as simple things often are—one of the best possible try-and-taste brunches you can give is a cheese-tasting party. What does it entail? A shopping trip, with one stop at the cheese store to buy a supply of very good cheese, one stop at the bakery to buy a supply of very good crusty bread, one stop at the greengrocer for a supply of fresh, ripe fruit. Make a simple dessert in advance, set up a buffet table, and your guests are on their own. If you'd like to see how into cheeses your guests are, make a game of it: Ask them to try each kind and see how many they can identify.

Smirnoff Martinis
Sharp Cheddar   *Mild Cheddar*
Edam or Gouda   *Gruyère*
Lager Käse Brick   *Camembert*
Fontina   *Neufchâtel*   *Roquefort*
Crusty White Bread   *Crusty Whole-Wheat Bread*
Dark, Firm-textured Rye Bread
Butter Crackers   *Sweet Butter*   *Sesame Crackers*
Fresh Pears   *Fresh Apples*
Dry Red Wine
Almond Slices   *Coffee*

SMIRNOFF MARTINI

1 drink

1¾ ounces Smirnoff Silver Vodka   **Pickled onion or lemon twist**
¼ ounce dry vermouth

Chill a 3-ounce cocktail glass. Fill martini pitcher with cracked ice. Measure ingredients for number of drinks required; pour in vodka first, then vermouth. Stir until drink is very cold. Strain into chilled glasses. Add onion or lemon twist.

ALMOND SLICES

2 dozens

2 eggs

1 cup light brown sugar,
firmly packed

1 square (1 ounce) unsweetened
chocolate, grated

1 cup unblanched almonds,
coarsely chopped

1 teaspoon baking powder

½ teaspoon cinnamon

2 cups sifted flour

1 teaspoon vanilla extract

Oil a 9-inch-square baking pan. Beat the eggs until light and then gradually add the sugar, beating well. Stir in the chocolate and almonds, then the dry ingredients, sifted together, and the vanilla. Mix well and press into the prepared pan. Bake in a preheated 350° oven for 25 minutes. Cool slightly and cut into strips.

FONDUE'S FUN

There's something essentially friendly about a fondue party—how can a group of people dip into the same pot and remain standoffish? For this occasion you'll need a number of fondue pots and/or chafing dishes, more than any normal household can be expected to have. Borrow—from people you invite to the brunch, of course! You'll also need a large supply of fondue forks (again, borrow) as well as a plate and an eat-with fork for each bruncher. Finger bowls are useful or have a supply—in the Oriental fashion—of hot, damp cloths. Each of the recipes in this section will serve four if used separately—for the purpose of this try-and-taste kind of brunch, each will serve eight to ten people very adequately.

Smirnoff and Guinness

Swiss Fondue *Rum Tum Tiddy*

Beef Fondue *Oriental Fondue*

Salsa Verde *Gentle Curry Sauce* *Onion Sauce*

Sauce Béarnaise

Assortment of Pickles and Relishes

Mocha Fondue

Coffee

SMIRNOFF AND GUINNESS

1 drink

1½ ounces Smirnoff Vodka   Guinness Stout

Pour vodka into a tall beer goblet. Fill with Guinness, pouring slowly to establish a good head.

SWISS FONDUE

8 small servings

1 pound Swiss cheese, finely diced
3 tablespoons flour
1 clove garlic
2 cups dry white wine
1 tablespoon lemon juice

½ cup Arrow Kirsch
⅛ teaspoon salt
¼ teaspoon white pepper
⅛ teaspoon nutmeg
Dippables

Place cheese in a bowl; sprinkle with flour and mix lightly. Cut garlic in half; rub inside of fondue pot with cut garlic; discard garlic. Pour wine into pot and place over low heat until bubbles start to rise to the surface—do not boil. Add lemon juice. Add cheese by handfuls, stirring constantly until cheese is melted. After last of cheese is added and melted, add kirsch and seasonings; stir to blend.

Dippables: Hard rolls, cut into bite-size pieces; cherry tomatoes; boiled new potatoes, halved.

RUM TUM TIDDY

1 can (10½ ounces) condensed
   tomato soup
½ pound sharp process American
   cheese, cubed

½ teaspoon dry mustard
8 slices bacon, cooked crisp
Dippables

Combine soup, cheese and dry mustard, and beat gently. Heat in chafing dish over hot water until cheese is melted. (If too thick, add a little milk or thin cream.) Crumble bacon over top and serve.
Dippables: Rye bread, toasted, cut into 1-inch squares; celery and green pepper chunks; cocktail onions.

BEEF FONDUE

8 small servings

2⅔ pounds lean sirloin
   or other tender beef

Cooking oil (salad or peanut oil)
Sauces

Cut meat into cubes of about ¾ inch each. Fill fondue pot with oil to about halfway and heat to the boiling point. Set pot over heating unit on serving table and place a small piece of bread in the bottom to prevent spattering. Guests spear 1 cube of meat at a time on a fondue fork and cook it in the hot oil to suit their individual tastes. When meat is done, guests transfer meat from fondue forks to table forks and dip it in the sauce of their choice.

ORIENTAL FONDUE

8 small servings

2⅔ pounds of meat
   Chicken bouillon

Sauces

Use one kind of meat or a combination, as you like—chicken, veal, calves' liver, sweetbreads and shellfish work well for this. Cut the meat into wafer-thin slices or cubes, as you prefer. If you do this at home, freeze the meats first—it makes the job much easier. Fill the pot two-thirds full of bouillon and bring to a boil; it must be kept boiling throughout the meal. Guests cook their own meat, as in Beef Fondue.
Idea: Meat is not the only food that can be cooked by the fondue method—try cauliflowerets, green pepper chunks, mushrooms, other vegetables.

SALSA VERDE

1 slice white bread
¼ cup white vinegar
½ teaspoon anchovy paste
1 cup finely snipped parsley
1½ teaspoons chopped capers

2 cloves garlic, crushed
1½ teaspoons grated onion
4 teaspoons olive oil
½ teaspoon sugar
2 tablespoons white vinegar

Remove crusts from bread; soak bread in vinegar. Combine with all remaining ingredients except vinegar. Beat to a smooth paste. Stir in vinegar and, if desired, more oil.

GENTLE CURRY SAUCE

1 small onion, chopped
1 small clove garlic, minced
1 piece (1 inch long) gingerroot,
   slivered
1 tablespoon butter

½ tablespoon curry powder
½ teaspoon dark brown sugar
1½ tablespoons flour
¼ teaspoon salt
1 cup chicken stock

Sauté onion, garlic and ginger in the butter until onion is lightly browned. Stir in curry and sugar; cook 1 minute. Stir in flour and salt. Gradually add chicken stock and cook, stirring until sauce is thickened. Cook over low heat 10 minutes, stirring frequently. Strain. Serve hot or cold.

ONION SAUCE

1 cup dairy sour cream
1 package (1½ ounces) dry
   onion-soup mix
3 egg yolks, beaten

1 teaspoon lemon juice
½ teaspoon Worcestershire sauce
   Salt and white pepper to taste

Blend sour cream and soup mix. Add remaining ingredients and cook over low heat, stirring constantly, until sauce starts to thicken. Do not boil. Cool before serving.

SAUCE BEARNAISE

¾ cup dry white wine
¼ cup tarragon vinegar
1 tablespoon finely chopped shallots
1 teaspoon snipped parsley
¼ teaspoon chopped fresh tarragon

¼ teaspoon thyme
   Few grains black pepper
3 egg yolks, slightly beaten
¾ cup melted butter

Combine all ingredients except egg yolks and butter in top of double boiler. Cook over direct heat until reduced by half. Cool. Place over hot water and add, alternately, a little at a time, the egg yolks and melted butter, beating all the while until of the consistency of lightly whipped cream.
Idea: Serve, as well, Hollandaise Sauce (see page 30), Grey Poupon mustard, and Escoffier Sauce Robert.

MOCHA FONDUE
                                        8 servings

20 ounces milk chocolate
1 cup heavy cream

2 tablespoons instant coffee powder
   Dippables

Break chocolate into pieces about 1 inch square and place in fondue pot. Add remaining ingredients and cook over low heat, stirring until chocolate is melted and mixture is smooth. Place over low heat to serve.
Dippables: Angel food cake, cut into 1-inch squares; marshmallows; bananas, sliced lengthwise and then cut into 1-inch chunks; whole strawberries; pineapple chunks; plain doughnuts, cut into eighths.

A BEVY OF OMELETS-PLUS

Here, to taste, to enjoy, are the "peasant" omelets of several countries. These are hearty fare, each one harboring savory surprises, each quite different from any of the others. Although some of these dishes are normally served folded, as a plain omelet is, this time turn out each, cut into wedge-shaped pieces, on a hot serving dish so that every bruncher can have a small portion of each omelet.

Smirnoff Bloody Marys (page 9)
French Omelet Savoyarde   Basque Piperade
American Farmer's Breakfast
Italian Frittata   Chinese Eggs Foo Yong
Toasted, Buttered English Muffins
Fresh Pineapple with Arrow White Crème de Menthe
Black-Walnut Crisps   Coffee

FRENCH OMELET SAVOYARDE
8 small servings

2 potatoes
1 tablespoon butter
¾ teaspoon onion juice
   Salt and white pepper to taste
2 leeks
2 tablespoons butter

5 eggs, slightly beaten
⅔ cup light cream
   Salt and pepper to taste
2 tablespoons snipped parsley
¼ cup grated Gruyère cheese

Wash the potatoes and cook in boiling salted water until tender but still firm. Cool, pare, cut in cubes. Melt 1 tablespoon butter in a small skillet. Add potato cubes and onion juice. Season lightly with salt and pepper. Cook until potatoes are lightly browned. Reserve. Meanwhile wash leeks, slice white parts only in crosswise slices and cook in boiling water until tender. Drain and reserve. Melt 2 tablespoons butter in an omelet pan. Mix eggs and cream and season lightly with salt and pepper. Pour into pan. Cook 3 minutes. Add potatoes, leeks and parsley. Continue to cook until creamy. Sprinkle with cheese, wait a moment until cheese is partially melted, and slide omelet out onto a heated serving dish.

BASQUE PIPERADE
8 small servings

3 tablespoons butter
3 onions, finely chopped
3 green peppers, seeded and
   finely diced
6 medium-size ripe tomatoes,
   peeled and quartered

   Salt and pepper to taste
1 tablespoon butter
5 eggs, lightly beaten
   Anchovy fillets

Melt 3 tablespoons butter in a saucepan. Add onions and peppers and cook until onions are yellow. Add tomatoes and cook over low heat until sauce is thick. Season to taste. Melt 1 tablespoon butter in an omelet pan. Add the eggs, then the tomato sauce; stir with a fork until omelet begins to set, then allow to cook without further stirring. Slide out onto a heated serving platter and garnish with anchovies placed spoke-fashion.

AMERICAN FARMER'S BREAKFAST
8 small servings

- 8 slices raw bacon, diced
- ½ cup minced onion
- ½ cup diced celery
- 1 cup diced, cooked potatoes
  Salt and pepper to taste
- 8 cooked brown-and-serve sausages, cut in small chunks
- 5 eggs
- ⅓ cup light cream
  Paprika

Fry bacon until crisp. Pour off all but about 3 tablespoons drippings. Add onion and celery and sauté 5 minutes. Add potatoes and cook until light brown, stirring occasionally. Sprinkle with salt and pepper. Stir in sausage chunks. Beat eggs with cream, just enough to blend, and pour into pan over vegetables. Cook, stirring lightly, until eggs are just set. Slide out onto heated serving platter and sprinkle with paprika.

ITALIAN FRITTATA
8 small servings

- ⅓ cup fine, dry bread crumbs
- ¼ cup tomato juice
- 1½ tablespoons olive oil
- 1 clove garlic
- 2 tablespoons minced onion
- 5 eggs, slightly beaten
- ¾ cup cooked green beans
- ¾ cup diced, cooked zucchini
- 1 tablespoon olive oil

Soak the crumbs in the tomato juice and reserve. Put 1½ tablespoons olive oil in a large skillet. Stick a toothpick into the garlic and place in skillet. Add onion and cook slowly until onion is pale yellow. Remove garlic and discard. Mix eggs, vegetables and crumbs. Place remaining 1 tablespoon olive oil in skillet; add egg mixture. Cover and cook slowly until frittata shrinks from sides of pan. If the center puffs up during cooking, prick with a fork. Slide out onto heated serving platter and cut into wedges to serve.

CHINESE EGGS FOO YONG
8 small servings

- 5 eggs
- ¼ cup slivered scallions
- ½ cup drained bean sprouts
- ½ cup chopped, cooked shrimp
- ½ cup sliced water chestnuts
- ½ cup sliced mushrooms
  Salt and pepper to taste
  Soy sauce
- 1 tablespoon butter

Beat eggs and ½ cup water together. Add scallions, bean sprouts, shrimp, water chestnuts and mushrooms. Season to taste with salt, pepper and soy sauce. Melt butter in a large omelet pan. Pour in egg mixture and brown on both sides. Slide out onto heated serving platter and cut into wedges.

BLACK-WALNUT CRISPS

5 dozens

1 cup butter, softened
2 cups light brown sugar,
  firmly packed
2 eggs
4 cups sifted flour

Pinch of salt
1 teaspoon baking powder
1 cup finely chopped,
  black-walnut meats

Cream butter and sugar. Add the eggs, 1 at a time, beating after each addition. Sift the flour, salt and baking powder together and beat into the first mixture. This will become very stiff. Work the nut meats in—using your hands if necessary. Shape the dough into a roll about 1½ inches in diameter. Wrap in waxed paper and chill in refrigerator overnight. Cut the roll into slices ⅛ inch thick and place them on an unoiled cookie sheet. Bake in a preheated 375° oven for 8 to 10 minutes, or until lightly browned. Cool on wire racks.

SOUP OF THE SUMMER, BEAUTIFUL SOUP!

There are more wonderful cold summer soups than you could crowd into a dozen brunch menus. Why not decide on four superb ones and invite friends to share them? Skip the too-usual vichyssoise and gazpacho—everyone serves those. Instead, offer these less familiar soups, which are blender-made. Four servings are about as much as a blender can accommodate, but since these soups are so easy to make, you won't mind blending two, even three or four, batches of each one, depending on the number of guests. This is an easy-on-the-hostess brunch, for the soups—as well as the accompaniments—can be made in advance. So can the dessert. All you need to do on the day of the party is set a pretty table. You'll need a lot of soup cups or small bowls. Again, borrow—that's what friends are for!

Smirnoff Lime Drys
Frosty Sour-Cream Tomato Soup   *Springtime Pea Soup*
Superb Asparagus Soup   *Blender Borsch*
Assorted Soup Garnishes
Chive-Cheese Finger Sandwiches   *Parsley-Butter Finger Sandwiches*
Superb Chocolate Mousse   *Florentines*
Coffee

SMIRNOFF LIME DRY

1 drink

1½ ounces Smirnoff Vodka
  Juice of ½ lime

½ teaspoon confectioners sugar
2 dashes orange bitters

Combine all ingredients and shake well with cracked ice. Strain into a 3-ounce glass.

FROSTY SOUR-CREAM TOMATO SOUP

4 servings

2 cans (10½ ounces each) condensed
tomato soup

1 cup dairy sour cream

Put soup, sour cream and 1½ cups water into blender container. Cover and process at medium speed until smooth. Chill at least several hours.

SPRINGTIME PEA SOUP

4 servings

1 package (10 ounces) frozen peas
1 cup chicken broth
1 large lettuce leaf, torn
into 4 pieces
1 tablespoon minced onion

½ teaspoon salt
¼ teaspoon white pepper
⅛ teaspoon ground cardamom
1 cup light or heavy cream

Break up frozen peas and place in blender container. Add broth, lettuce, onion and seasonings. Cover and process at medium speed for 1 minute. Add cream and process at low speed 20 seconds. Chill at least 2 hours.

SUPERB ASPARAGUS SOUP

4 servings

1 package (10 ounces) frozen
asparagus
1 cup chicken broth
2 mushrooms, quartered
1 tablespoon minced onion

½ teaspoon salt
¼ teaspoon chili powder
½ teaspoon lemon juice
1 cup light or heavy cream

Break up frozen asparagus and place in blender container. Add all remaining ingredients except cream. Cover and process at medium speed for 1 minute. Add cream; process at low speed 30 seconds. Chill.

BLENDER BORSCH

4 servings

1 cup dairy sour cream
1 cup beef bouillon
½ small lemon, peeled and seeded
¼ teaspoon salt

¼ teaspoon celery salt
½ teaspoon dried dillweed
1 cup diced, cooked beets

Combine all ingredients in blender container. Cover and process at medium speed for 1 minute, or until smooth. Serve ice cold.

ASSORTED SOUP GARNISHES

Parsley
Bacon, cooked crisp
Dairy sour cream
Snipped chives

Peanuts
Scallions
Dill pickles
Croutons

Snip parsley, crumble bacon, sprinkle sour cream with chives, chop peanuts, chop scallions, chop dill pickles. Put each garnish into a separate dish and let your guests help themselves to whatever they like.

CHIVE-CHEESE FINGER SANDWICHES

For each serving use 2 slices of square, firm-type white bread and 1½ ta-blespoons chive cheese. (Use packaged chived cream cheese or mix your own, using whipped cream cheese and fresh chives.) Spread 1 slice of bread with cheese, salt lightly, top with the second slice; trim crusts and cut sandwich into 3 finger-shaped pieces.

PARSLEY-BUTTER FINGER SANDWICHES

For each serving use 2 slices of square, firm-type whole-wheat or rye bread and 1½ tablespoons butter creamed with 2 teaspoons finely snipped parsley and 2 drops lemon juice. Spread 1 slice with parsley butter, top with second slice; trim crusts and cut into 3 finger-shaped pieces.

FLORENTINES
4 dozens

¼ cup butter
¼ cup light brown sugar,
  firmly packed
1 tablespoon honey
½ cup sifted flour
½ cup candied fruits, cut finely

½ cup candied lemon and orange peels, cut finely
¼ cup chopped seedless raisins
½ cup almonds, ground
1 package (6 ounces) semisweet chocolate bits, melted

Oil a cookie sheet. Melt the butter and add the sugar and honey. Sift the flour over the fruits and nuts and add to the butter-sugar mixture. Mix well. Spoon small amounts onto the prepared cookie sheet and flatten each with a wet metal spatula. Bake in a preheated 350° oven for 8 to 10 min-utes, or until the cookies are browned around the edges. Cool on a wire rack. When cold, spread the bottoms with the melted chocolate.

SUPERB CHOCOLATE MOUSSE
4 servings

1 package (6 ounces) semisweet chocolate bits
2 eggs
3 tablespoons strong, hot coffee

1 to 2 tablespoons rum, brandy or Arrow Curaçao
¾ cup milk, scalded

Combine all ingredients in blender. Cover and process at high speed for 2 minutes. Pour into 4 dessert dishes and refrigerate at least 4 hours before serving.

BONUS: ALL ABOUT SALADS AND DRESSINGS

Perhaps you are one of those people who feel a meal is not a meal without a salad—or perhaps your husband is. You can add a salad to almost any menu in this book that does not call for one, anything from sliced tomatoes with a good dressing through a wedge of lettuce nicely dressed or a tossed green salad to a refreshing fruit salad that augments, or doubles for, dessert. Here are salad dressings of several kinds, with comments on what they dress best.

French Dressing (Sauce Vinaigrette): In a small bowl combine ¼ teaspoon each of salt and pepper, 1 tablespoon olive oil, 1 tablespoon red or white wine vinegar or lemon juice and (if you like) 1 teaspoon dry mustard. Beat with a fork until well combined. Add 2 tablespoons olive oil and beat again. Add 1 tablespoon vinegar or lemon juice and 3 tablespoons olive oil. Here, if you like, add 1 peeled garlic clove. Place the dressing in a jar, well-covered, and refrigerate. Shake well before using on mixed greens or on cold vegetables, such as sliced tomatoes, asparagus, mushrooms, or a mélange of mixed vegetables. This makes about ½ cup of dressing.

Fruit-Salad French Dressing: For the vinegar in French Dressing, substitute 3 tablespoons grapefruit juice.

Cream-Cheese Dressing: Mash one 3-ounce package of cream cheese with a fork; beat until smooth. Add 2 teaspoons minced chives, ½ teaspoon dry mustard, 1 teaspoon salt, ½ teaspoon white pepper; mix well. Gradually beat in ¼ cup salad oil and 1½ tablespoons cider vinegar. Use with a green or vegetable salad.

Bleu-Cheese Dressing: Into ½ cup of French Dressing, beat 3 tablespoons crumbled bleu cheese. Serve on mixed greens or lettuce wedge.

Green Goddess Dressing: With 1 cup mayonnaise, combine 1 minced garlic clove, 3 minced anchovy fillets, ¼ cup finely chopped scallions, ¼ cup minced parsley, 1 tablespoon lemon juice, 1 tablespoon tarragon vinegar, ¼ teaspoon salt. Mix in ½ cup sour cream. For greens, fish or shellfish.

Thousand Island Dressing: Into 1 cup of mayonnaise, beat 3 tablespoons catsup, ½ teaspoon Worcestershire sauce, 2 tablespoons grated onion, 2 tablespoons well-drained sweet pickle relish, 2 chopped hard-cooked eggs (page 137), 1 tablespoon snipped parsley. Dresses up a plain wedge of lettuce; fine with shrimp or crab or egg dishes of any kind.

Double Dressing: Into 1 cup of mayonnaise, stir 1 cup French Dressing, 1 minced garlic clove, 1 teaspoon anchovy paste, ¼ cup grated Romano cheese. Use to dress hearts of lettuce.

Russian Dressing: Into 1 cup of mayonnaise, stir 1 tablespoon drained horseradish, 1 teaspoon Worcestershire sauce, ¼ cup chili sauce, 1 teaspoon grated onion. If you want to make it even more authentically Russian, add 3 tablespoons caviar. Use on cold vegetable salads or on chicken or fish or shellfish—delicious on shrimp.

Curry Dressing: Mix 2 tablespoons white wine vinegar, 1 tablespoon lemon juice, ½ teaspoon curry powder, 1 teaspoon sugar. Stir into 1 cup dairy sour cream. This is surprisingly good on almost any fruit salad.

Old-fashioned Boiled Dressing: In a heavy saucepan, lightly beat 2 eggs with a fork. Stir in ½ cup sugar, 4 tablespoons flour, 1 teaspoon onion powder, ½ teaspoon turmeric, 1 teaspoon salt and a few grains of cayenne until well blended. Add 1 cup cider vinegar, then 2 cups milk. Cook, stirring, over low heat until the mixture bubbles and thickens. Makes a great cole slaw, a wonderful "down home" sort of potato salad, and a Pennsylvania Dutch wilted lettuce superior to any other. Store tightly covered in the refrigerator. Keeps about 2 weeks.

Red-Caviar Dressing: Into 1 cup dairy sour cream, stir 1 teaspoon onion juice and 2 teaspoons well-drained capers. Gently stir in 4 tablespoons red caviar. Makes a plain cooked vegetable salad about as dressy as it can get; wonderful on hot baked potatoes or as a dip for crudités.

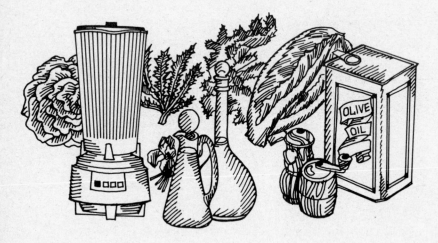

THE PATIO BRUNCH

PLAY AND PIZZAS

Brunch outside makes the day seem very special. The air, the sun, the soaring birds and the blue sky give the scene an air of well-being. Today is special, the day for flying saucers, not only in the air, but for brunch too. While the guests are enjoying Smirnoff Sours and nibbles, and flying frisbees all over the backyard, put the finishing touches to your own version of flying saucers—pizzas!

Smirnoff Sours (page 33)
Black-Bean Dip   Round Crackers and Corn Chips
Mushrooms a la Grecque
Pepperoni Pizza   Cheese Pizza
Mushroom-and-Cheese Pizza
Vanilla Ice-Cream Balls
Best Chocolate Sauce
Coffee

BLACK-BEAN DIP
2½ cups

1 can (10½ ounces) condensed
    black-bean soup, undiluted
1 can (8 ounces) tomato sauce

½ to 1 cup shredded
    sharp Cheddar cheese
¼ teaspoon chili powder

Combine soup, tomato sauce, ½ cup of the cheese and chili powder in saucepan. Cook at medium heat until the cheese has melted. Add more shredded cheese until the mixture is as thick as desired. Serve from electric skillet or saucepan kept warm on an electric trivet or candle. Serve with crackers or corn chips.

MUSHROOMS A LA GRECQUE
8 servings

1 pound small mushrooms
    Juice of 1 lemon
1½ teaspoons salt
½ teaspoon freshly ground
    black pepper

2 tablespoons olive oil
2 teaspoons Grey Poupon mustard
2 tablespoons snipped parsley

Wash, pat dry and trim mushrooms, but leave whole. Place in a small saucepan with lemon juice, salt, pepper and oil. Cover and simmer for 10 minutes. Let stand until cool. Chill in refrigerator. Scoop out mushrooms from marinade with a slotted spoon and place in a serving dish. Blend mustard with marinade. Pour over mushrooms. Sprinkle with parsley.

PIZZA CRUST
2 crusts

1 package or cake yeast,
active dry or compressed
2½ cups sifted flour

1 teaspoon salt
1 tablespoon salad oil

In large mixer bowl, combine yeast, 1 cup of the flour and salt. Add 1 cup warm water and the oil. Beat with electric mixer set at low speed for ½ minute, scraping sides of bowl. Beat at high speed for 3 minutes. By hand, stir in enough of the remaining flour to make a stiff dough. Turn out on a lightly floured board and knead until smooth and elastic, 8 to 10 minutes. Place in an oiled bowl, turning once to oil surface. Cover and let rise in a warm place, free from draft, until more than doubled in bulk, about 1½ hours. Punch down; cover and place in refrigerator for 2 hours. Cut dough in half. On floured surface, roll each half to a circle about 12 inches in diameter. Place on 2 oiled 12-inch pizza pans. Crimp edges. Brush with oil. Top according to taste or with any of the toppings given in the following recipes. Bake in a preheated 425° oven for 20 to 25 minutes, or until browned.

PEPPERONI PIZZA
2 pizzas

1 can (15 ounces) tomato sauce
½ cup minced onion
2 teaspoons oregano
2 cloves garlic, minced

Dash of pepper
½ pound pepperoni, very
thinly sliced
½ pound shredded mozzarella cheese

Prepare 2 pizza crusts. Combine tomato sauce, onion, oregano, garlic and pepper. Spread half of the mixture evenly over each pizza crust. Scatter pepperoni over each top. Sprinkle with cheese. Bake in a preheated 425° oven for 20 to 25 minutes, or until crust is brown, filling bubbly.

CHEESE PIZZA
2 pizzas

1 can (15 ounces) tomato sauce
1 tablespoon minced onion
½ teaspoon oregano
½ teaspoon salt

¼ teaspoon pepper
½ cup grated Parmesan cheese
½ pound thinly sliced
mozzarella cheese

Prepare 2 pizza crusts. Combine tomato sauce, minced onion, oregano, salt and pepper. Spread half of the mixture evenly over each pizza crust. Sprinkle each with Parmesan cheese. Arrange slices of mozzarella cheese on top. Bake in a preheated 425° oven for 20 to 25 minutes, or until crust is brown and filling is bubbly.

MUSHROOM-AND-CHEESE PIZZA

2 pizzas

½ cup chopped onion
1 clove garlic, minced
2 tablespoons salad oil
1 can (6 ounces) sliced mushrooms
1 can (6 ounces) tomato paste
2 teaspoons light brown sugar,
  firmly packed

1 teaspoon basil
1 teaspoon oregano
½ teaspoon salt
¼ teaspoon pepper
½ cup grated Parmesan cheese
6 ounces mozzarella cheese,
  cut in thin strips

Prepare 2 pizza crusts. Cook onion and garlic in hot salad oil until tender but not browned. Stir in undrained mushrooms, tomato paste, sugar, basil, oregano, salt and pepper. Heat, stirring occasionally. Spread evenly over each pizza crust. Sprinkle with Parmesan cheese. Bake in a preheated 425° oven for 20 minutes. Remove from oven; top with mozzarella cheese. Bake 3 to 5 minutes.

BEST CHOCOLATE SAUCE

2 cups sauce

1 package (12 ounces)
  semisweet chocolate bits
2 squares (2 ounces)
  unsweetened chocolate

1 cup heavy cream
3 tablespoons brandy

Melt chocolate in top of double boiler over hot water. Stir in cream with a wire whisk to make a smooth mixture. Stir in brandy. Serve hot over vanilla ice cream.

GO FLY A KITE

Come spring and the beginning of summer, everyone wants to get out of doors. Everyone else is as tired of being cooped up inside the house as you are, so why not invite friends for the first outdoor feast of the year? A brunch is ideal for eating outdoors early in the season, with the sun for a bit of warmth and with games to play—perhaps the first baseball game of the year or, if weather permits, a day of kite-flying. Have hearty food—a choice of two good hot soups with crusty bread to go with them—and for dessert, a substantial cheesecake and lots of coffee.

Smirnoff Storms
Hearty Party Soup
Cioppino
Cheddar Bread Sticks   *Buttered French Bread*
Cheesecake Melba
Coffee

SMIRNOFF STORM

1 drink

Shaved ice
2 ounces (about) Smirnoff Vodka

1 cocktail olive

Fill sours glass with shaved ice. Pour in vodka to fill. Add olive. Serve with short straws.

HEARTY PARTY SOUP

10 servings

1 large soup bone, split
2 pounds soup meat
1 tablespoon salt
½ medium-size cabbage, sliced
2 onions, chopped
6 carrots, pared and cut in
   3-inch pieces
2 stalks celery, cut up
¼ green pepper, seeded and cut up
1 can (1 pound, 13 ounces) tomatoes

1 cup cut green beans
1 cup peas
1 can (12 ounces) whole-kernel corn
1 potato, peeled and cubed
2 tablespoons snipped parsley
½ cup catsup
1 teaspoon sugar
1 teaspoon salt
¼ teaspoon pepper

Place soup bone, soup meat and salt in a large kettle with 4 quarts water. Bring to a boil and simmer 20 minutes. Skim off any foam that rises to the top of soup. Add cabbage, onions, carrots, celery, pepper and tomatoes. Simmer, covered, about 30 minutes. Add remaining ingredients. Simmer, covered, about 2 hours. Taste for seasoning. Remove meat and bone from soup. Cut up pieces of meat and return to soup. Cool soup by setting kettle in ice water. Skim all fat from top of soup. Reheat slowly just before serving. Serve piping hot.

CIOPPINO

8 servings

1 large onion, chopped
1 medium-size green pepper,
   seeded and chopped
½ cup sliced celery
1 carrot, pared and shredded
3 cloves garlic, minced
3 tablespoons olive oil
2 cans (1 pound each) tomatoes
1 can (8 ounces) tomato sauce
1 teaspoon crumbled basil

1 bay leaf
1 teaspoon salt
¼ teaspoon pepper
1 pound white fish
1 dozen mussels *or* littleneck
   clams in the shells
1½ cups dry white wine
½ pound shrimp, cleaned
½ pound scallops
Snipped parsley

Cook onion, green pepper, celery, carrot and garlic in olive oil in a dutch oven until soft. Stir in tomatoes, tomato sauce, basil, bay leaf, salt and pepper. Heat to boiling. Reduce heat, cover and simmer 2 hours. Discard bay leaf. While sauce is simmering, cut white fish into serving pieces. Using a stiff brush, thoroughly scrub the mussels, cutting off their beards, or soak clams in cold water to which cornmeal has been added and then scrub under running water to remove any residue of mud and sand. Stir wine into tomato mixture. Add white fish, shrimp and scallops. Cover and simmer 10 minutes. Place mussels or clams in a layer on top of fish in kettle. Cover and steam 5 to 10 minutes, or until the shells are fully opened. Discard any mussels or clams that are unopened. Ladle soup into soup plates or bowls. Sprinkle with parsley.

CHEDDAR BREAD STICKS

2 dozens

1 package or cake yeast,
  active dry or compressed
1 tablespoon sugar
1½ teaspoons salt
½ cup finely shredded sharp
  Cheddar cheese

3 cups flour
  Melted butter
1 egg white
  Coarse salt *or*
  caraway seeds

Measure 1¼ cups warm (105°-115°) water into a large warm bowl. Sprinkle or crumble in yeast; stir until dissolved. Add sugar, salt, cheese and enough flour to make a soft dough. Turn out on a lightly floured board; knead until smooth and elastic, about 10 minutes. Place in an oiled bowl and turn dough over to oil top. Cover and let rise in a warm place, free from draft, until doubled in bulk, about 35 minutes. Punch down; turn out on a lightly floured board and cut in half. Roll each half into an oblong 9 x 12 inches. Cut into twelve 3-inch squares. Brush lightly with melted butter. Roll up, jelly-roll fashion. Place on an unoiled baking sheet. Cover and let rise in a warm place, free from draft, until doubled in bulk, about 30 minutes. Brush with egg white that has been beaten lightly with 1 tablespoon water. Sprinkle with coarse salt or caraway seeds. Bake in a preheated 400° oven for 15 to 20 minutes, or until golden brown. Cool.

CHEESECAKE MELBA

12 to 16 servings

18 single graham crackers
⅓ cup butter, melted
⅛ teaspoon cinnamon
  Dash of nutmeg
3 large eggs
¾ cup sugar

3 packages (8 ounces each)
  cream cheese, at room temperature
1 teaspoon vanilla extract
2 cups dairy sour cream
⅓ cup sugar
1 teaspoon vanilla extract

Oil the bottom of a 9-inch springform pan. Place crackers in a plastic bag and crush with a rolling pin. Pour into a bowl. Add butter, cinnamon and nutmeg; blend thoroughly. Press firmly on bottom of springform pan. Beat eggs with mixer at low speed until well blended. Gradually add ¾ cup sugar and beat until thickened. Cut cream cheese in chunks and add gradually to mixture. Continue beating until mixture is very smooth. Add 1 teaspoon vanilla. Pour into springform pan. Bake in a preheated 350° oven for 45 minutes, or until cake is fairly firm. Remove cake from oven. Turn oven up to 450°. Combine sour cream, ⅓ cup sugar and 1 teaspoon vanilla. Spread gently over top of cheesecake. Bake 4 to 5 minutes, or just until topping is set. Remove from oven and cool on wire rack. Refrigerate overnight before serving.

ANY DAY IS FATHER'S DAY

Choose any day to be Father's Day—the day he functions as chef. Set up a beautiful brunch table on the porch or patio. Have electric hot plates or small outdoor camping stoves ready to use, with omelet pans and all ingredients waiting. As guests get hungry, let father show off his skill as a cook—or all the fathers may want to have a hand in proving their cooking prowess. Finish the brunch with homemade cinnamon coffee braid and lots of strong, hot coffee.

Smirnoff Bloody Marys (page 9)
Made-to-Order Omelets
Crab Filling   Tomato Filling
Toasted, Buttered Hard Rolls
Western Sun Salad   Cinnamon Coffee Braid
Coffee

MADE-TO-ORDER OMELETS   8 servings

10 eggs
¾ teaspoon salt

¼ teaspoon pepper
¼ cup butter, divided

Combine eggs, salt, pepper and ¼ cup water. Beat lightly with a fork, just until yolks and whites are combined. Heat 1 tablespoon of butter in an omelet pan over high heat just until butter begins to turn brown. Add one-quarter of the egg mixture and immediately stir briskly with a fork. When eggs have thickened, stop stirring. With left hand, shake the pan gently back and forth to loosen eggs and brown the bottom gently. Remove skillet from heat and tip it gently. With a fork, fold one-third of omelet over center. Then fold other third over first. Slide omelet out of pan onto a heated serving dish and cut in half. Repeat three more times.

Try this way: When eggs have just set, sprinkle 1 to 2 tablespoons grated Swiss or Cheddar cheese over top and finish omelet as recipe directs.

CRAB FILLING

4 servings

1 pound crab meat
1 tablespoon butter
½ cup heavy cream
Pinch of salt

Dash of cayenne
1 tablespoon Cognac
1 tablespoon snipped chives

Break crab meat into small chunks and remove any shell or cartilage. Melt butter in a small skillet. Add crab and cream and warm gently. Add salt, cayenne, Cognac and chives. Heat gently and keep warm. Using a slotted spoon, fill center of each omelet with crab meat, then pour some of the sauce over top of finished omelet on serving plate.

TOMATO FILLING

4 servings

4 slices bacon
3 ripe tomatoes
½ teaspoon salt
½ teaspoon basil

Pinch of sugar
Dash of Tabasco sauce
½ teaspoon curry powder
Snipped parsley

Fry bacon until fairly crisp. Remove bacon to paper towels to drain. Peel, seed and cut up tomatoes. Add to bacon fat in skillet and cook, stirring occasionally, for about 30 minutes. Add salt, basil, sugar, Tabasco and the bacon, broken into pieces. Simmer 3 minutes. Stir in curry powder. Prepare omelets according to recipe. Before folding over, add a spoonful of tomato filling to center. Top with some additional tomato filling and sprinkle with snipped parsley.

WESTERN SUN SALAD

6 to 8 servings

¼ pound bleu cheese, crumbled
¾ teaspoon salad oil
1 teaspoon grated lemon peel
3 tablespoons lemon juice
1 cup dairy sour cream

½ teaspoon seasoned salt
6 navel oranges, peeled and cut
  into bite-size pieces
1½ quarts assorted, chilled
  salad greens

Combine bleu cheese, oil, lemon peel and juice in a small deep bowl. Beat with an electric mixer until smooth. Add sour cream and salt and mix well. Cover and chill at least 1 hour to blend flavors and mellow. Place orange sections and salad greens in a large bowl. Add dressing and toss lightly just before serving.

CINNAMON COFFEE BRAID

2 braids

¾ cup milk
¼ cup sugar
1½ teaspoons salt
1 cup butter
2 packages or cakes yeast,
  active dry or compressed

3 egg yolks, well beaten
4¼ cups flour
½ cup sugar
2 teaspoons cinnamon
¼ cup butter, melted

Scald milk. Stir in ¼ cup sugar, salt and 1 cup butter. Cool to lukewarm. Measure ½ cup warm (105°-115°) water into a large warm bowl. Sprinkle or crumble in yeast; stir until dissolved. Add lukewarm milk mixture and beaten egg yolks; stir to blend. Add flour; beat until well blended. Cover tightly with aluminum foil. Refrigerate at least 4 hours or overnight. Combine ½ cup sugar and cinnamon until well blended. Turn dough out onto a lightly floured board; divide in half. Divide each half into 3 pieces. Roll each piece into an 18-inch strand. Braid 3 pieces together; seal ends. Place on oiled baking sheet. Brush with melted butter and sprinkle with cinnamon-sugar mixture. Repeat with remaining 3 pieces of dough. Cover and let rise in a warm place, free from draft, until doubled in bulk, about 1 hour. Bake in a preheated 400° oven for 25 minutes, or until done. Cool.

NEIGHBORLY FUN

Have a big backyard party to celebrate the Fourth of July, Memorial Day or Labor Day. Or just have a party to celebrate "nothing." Invite all the neighbors and have each one contribute a part of the brunch. Because it is such a wonderful summer day, set up the badminton net or maybe an old-fashioned game of horseshoes, but because everyone is exercising and the day is glorious, have plenty of food and drink and good friendship.

Smirnoff and Tonics (page 66)
Clam Dip with Crisp Vegetables
Oven-fried Chicken   Cold Glazed Ham
Savory Potato Salad
Spicy Fruit Mold
Onion Rolls   Butter
Swedish Apple Cake
Coffee

CLAM DIP WITH CRISP VEGETABLES

2 cups

2 packages (3 ounces each) cream cheese
1 teaspoon salt
½ teaspoon Tabasco sauce
1 tablespoon grated onion
1 can (7½ ounces) minced clams
1 cup dairy sour cream

Place cream cheese in a small bowl and let soften at room temperature. Blend in salt, Tabasco and onion. Drain clams, reserving 2 teaspoons of the clam liquor. Add clams and the reserved liquor to cream cheese. Stir in sour cream and blend well. Turn into a serving dish and chill at least ½ hour before serving. Serve with crisp sticks of celery, cucumber, white turnip, carrot, small whole scallions and blades of Belgian endive.

OVEN-FRIED CHICKEN

4 to 6 servings

¾ cup cracker crumbs
⅓ cup grated Parmesan cheese
2 tablespoons snipped chives
2 tablespoons snipped parsley

1 broiler-fryer chicken, 3 to
  3½ pounds, cut in serving pieces
¼ cup butter, melted

Combine cracker crumbs, cheese, chives and parsley on a square of waxed paper. Dip pieces of chicken in melted butter and coat with crumb mixture. Place in a shallow roasting pan. Do not overlap chicken pieces. Bake in a preheated 375° oven for 45 minutes, or until chicken is tender.

COLD GLAZED HAM

6 to 8 servings

1 canned ham
1½ envelopes unflavored gelatin
½ cup cold chicken broth
¼ cup butter
¼ cup flour

2 cups milk
¼ teaspoon pepper
3 tablespoons dry sherry
1 can (4 ounces) pimientos

Have meat dealer slice ham into serving pieces and then reassemble in original shape. Place ham on a wire cake rack. Sprinkle gelatin on cold broth and let stand to soften. Melt butter in a saucepan. Stir in flour and blend well. Remove from heat. Stir in milk. Cook over medium heat, stirring constantly, until smooth and thickened. Remove from heat and stir in pepper and sherry. Add softened gelatin and stir until dissolved. Cool sauce. "Frost" the top and sides of the ham with sauce, using a broad knife or thin spatula. Garnish top with pimiento, cut into shapes as desired, and refrigerate immediately.

SAVORY POTATO SALAD

6 servings

6 medium-size potatoes,
  cooked and peeled
½ teaspoon savory
¼ teaspoon marjoram
2 teaspoons salt
¼ teaspoon pepper
1 tablespoon caraway seeds
¼ cup salad oil

¼ cup cider vinegar
1 medium-size onion, minced
½ cup mayonnaise
2 teaspoons Grey Poupon mustard
3 hard-cooked eggs (page 137),
  shelled
Lettuce leaves
Tomato quarters

Slice or dice potatoes into a large bowl. Put seasonings into a jar with the oil and vinegar; shake to blend well. Pour mixture over the potatoes and let stand about 1 hour. Add onion, mayonnaise and mustard. Dice 2 of the hard-cooked eggs and add to the potato mixture. Toss gently to combine all ingredients thoroughly. Serve on lettuce leaves and garnish with tomato quarters and remaining egg, sliced.

SPICY FRUIT MOLD

8 servings

1 can (1 pound) cling peach halves
1 can (13½ ounces) pineapple chunks
1 can (10 ounces) mandarin
   orange sections
1 stick (4 inches) cinnamon
½ teaspoon whole cloves
½ teaspoon allspice

1 package (6 ounces)
   lemon-flavored gelatin
⅔ cup dry white wine
3 tablespoons white wine vinegar
½ cup halved, seeded Tokay grapes
   Crisp salad greens

Drain syrup from peaches, pineapple and oranges into a saucepan. Add spices and simmer 10 minutes. Strain, measure liquid and add enough water to make 2½ cups liquid. Heat to simmering. Add gelatin and stir until dissolved. Add wine and vinegar. Cool until gelatin starts to thicken and jell. Fold in all fruits and turn into a 6½-cup mold. Chill for several hours or overnight. Unmold and garnish with crisp greens.

SWEDISH APPLE CAKE

8 to 10 servings

1 cup butter
⅓ cup sugar
1¾ cups sifted flour
½ cup zwieback crumbs
½ teaspoon salt
2 cups applesauce
½ cup light brown sugar,
   firmly packed

1 teaspoon cinnamon
1 teaspoon grated lemon peel
2 eggs, separated
¼ cup light brown sugar,
   firmly packed
¼ teaspoon salt
1 cup raspberry jam
½ cup slivered, blanched almonds

Combine butter, sugar, flour, crumbs and ½ teaspoon salt to make a crumbly dough. Measure ⅔ cup of this mixture and spread in a small pan. Press remaining mixture firmly in an oiled 12- x 8- x 2-inch pan. Bake this crust in a preheated 375° oven for 20 minutes, or until golden brown. At the same time, bake the small pan of crumbs 10 to 12 minutes, or until lightly browned. Combine applesauce, ½ cup brown sugar, cinnamon, lemon peel and the egg yolks in a saucepan. Cook over low heat, stirring constantly, until thickened, about 12 to 15 minutes. Beat egg whites until stiff. Gradually beat in ¼ cup brown sugar and ¼ teaspoon salt. Beat until this meringue is very stiff. Spread applesauce mixture over baked crust. Sprinkle with toasted crumbs. Spoon jam over top of crumbs. Spread meringue carefully over top. Sprinkle with almonds. Bake in a preheated 400° oven for 4 to 6 minutes, or until meringue is lightly browned. Cool and cut into squares to serve.

BRUNCH IT YOURSELF

Here are more good-for-brunch dishes—around which you can build your own, suit-yourself brunch.

SMIRNOFF HUNTSMAN   1 drink

1½ ounces Smirnoff Vodka   Juice of ½ lime
 ½ ounce Don Q White Rum   1 teaspoon confectioners sugar

Shake together ingredients with cracked ice. Strain into a chilled cocktail glass.

SMIRNOFF QUENCHER   1 drink

1½ ounces Smirnoff Vodka   Lemon-lime soda

Pour vodka over ice cubes in a tall glass. Fill with soda. Stir gently.

SMIRNOFF GIBSON   1 drink

 2 ounces Smirnoff Vodka   Cocktail onion
 ¾ ounce dry vermouth

In a cocktail shaker stir vodka and vermouth well with cracked ice. Pour into a chilled cocktail glass and add onion.

SUPERB CHICKEN HASH   4 to 6 servings

1 large onion, minced   Dash of Tabasco sauce
1 green pepper, seeded and diced   1 teaspoon tarragon
3 tablespoons butter   ¼ cup snipped parsley
1 tablespoon oil   ½ cup blanched, slivered almonds
2 cups coarsely diced,   6 eggs, slightly beaten
   cooked chicken or turkey   ½ cup grated Parmesan cheese

Using a large skillet, cook onion and pepper in heated butter and oil just until tender. Add chicken and toss lightly. Add Tabasco, tarragon, parsley and almonds and blend lightly. Press mixture down in skillet, cover and heat 2 to 3 minutes. Stop at this point and finish hash at the last minute, just before serving. Reheat mixture and proceed as follows. Combine eggs and cheese. Pour over chicken mixture; cook and stir over low heat until eggs are just set. Place skillet under preheated broiler for 2 to 3 minutes, or until mixture is just lightly browned on top. Serve immediately.

BAKED BEEF HASH   8 servings

3 cups cooked, cubed beef   1 tablespoon Worcestershire sauce
2 cups cooked, peeled and   2 teaspoons salt
   cubed potatoes   ¼ teaspoon pepper
1 can (13 ounces) evaporated milk ½ cup crushed saltine crackers
½ cup finely snipped parsley   2 tablespoons butter, melted
½ cup minced onion

Lightly toss together beef, potatoes, evaporated milk, parsley, onion, Worcestershire sauce, salt and pepper. Turn into a lightly oiled, shallow 2-quart casserole. Toss together cracker crumbs and melted butter. Sprinkle around the edges of hash. Bake uncovered in a preheated 350° oven for 30 minutes, or until mixture is hot and bubbly.

FRENCH-FRIED HAM SANDWICHES
25 sandwiches

- 6 eggs, well beaten
- 3 cups milk
- 1½ teaspoons salt
- 50 slices white bread
- ½ cup butter, softened
- ¼ cup Grey Poupon mustard
- 25 slices boiled ham
- 25 slices process American cheese

Combine eggs, milk and salt in a bowl until well blended. Spread 25 slices of bread with butter and mustard. Top each with a slice of ham and a slice of cheese. Cover with another slice of bread. Cut in half. Dip each half in egg mixture. Fry on a lightly oiled preheated griddle, in an electric skillet or in a cast-iron skillet over an outdoor barbecue until lightly browned on both sides.

TOASTED CHEESE SANDWICHES
25 sandwiches

- 2 packages (8 ounces each) cream cheese
- ¼ pound bleu cheese, crumbled
- 2 tablespoons minced onion
- 1 teaspoon salt
- ¼ cup butter, softened
- 50 slices whole-wheat bread

Allow cream cheese to soften at room temperature. Stir into bleu cheese. Add onion and salt and mix until well blended. Butter one side of each bread slice. Spread cheese mixture on other side. Sandwich together with buttered side out. Cut in half. Place sandwiches on a preheated griddle, in an electric skillet or in a cast-iron skillet over an outdoor barbecue. Cook until sandwiches are nicely browned on both sides.

ZESTY GARDEN DIP
1 cup

- 1 package (3 ounces) cream cheese, at room temperature
- ¼ cup mayonnaise
- 3 tablespoons dairy sour cream
- 2 tablespoons grated cucumber
- 2 tablespoons grated radishes
- ¼ teaspoon grated onion
- ¼ teaspoon dry mustard
- Salt and pepper to taste

Combine all ingredients and salt and pepper to taste. Blend thoroughly. Cover and chill. Serve with assorted crackers.

BRUNCH AROUND THE WORLD

THE MEXICAN WAY

Why not a trip around the world in the comfort of your own home? For a starter, a South-of-the-Border trip—to Mexico—for this delicious brunch. Use pottery dishes if you have or can borrow them and those wonderful, huge, extravagantly colored Mexican tissue-paper flowers for decoration. Nothing on this menu is hard to make—just a little difficult to pronounce, that's all. Most of it can be cooked in advance, served as is or heated at the last minute. Mexicans are warm, friendly, happy to have guests in their home—giving this brunch will make you feel the same way!

Smirnoff Margarettas
Queso Relleno   *Tortilla Chips*
Huevos de los Charros   *Pescado en Jugo de Naranja*
Frijoles con Platanos   *Molletes de Calabaza*
Ensalada de Calabacitas
Queso de Almendras   *Apples*
Chocolate Mexicano   *Coffee*

SMIRNOFF MARGARETTA
1 drink

1½ ounces Smirnoff Vodka
½ ounce Arrow Triple Sec
  Juice of ½ lime

Crushed ice
Lime peel
Salt

Stir vodka, Triple Sec and lime juice with crushed ice. Rub rim of 3-ounce cocktail glass with peel of lime; dip rim in salt; pour and serve.

QUESO RELLENO
(Stuffed Cheese)

8 servings

1 large Edam cheese
2 tablespoons shortening
½ pound ground pork
¼ pound ground beef (all pork or all beef may be used)
½ green pepper, seeded and chopped
Salt and pepper to taste
2 teaspoons tomato purée
Dash of onion juice
¼ cup drained capers
¼ cup ripe olives, pitted and chopped
¼ cup white raisins
¼ cup blanched almonds, coarsely chopped
1 tablespoon cinnamon
¼ cup snipped parsley
2 tablespoons dry white wine
5 hard-cooked eggs (page 137), chopped
¼ cup flour
1 sheet heavy parchment paper, lightly oiled

Place the cheese in lukewarm water for a few minutes to facilitate the removal of the red covering. Remove the covering. Cut a thin slice off the top of the cheese and reserve. Scrape out cheese until it resembles a bowl with ½-inch thickness around the outside. Heat the shortening and brown the meat in it along with the green pepper and salt and pepper. Blend tomato purée with dash of onion juice; add this along with capers, olives, raisins, almonds, and cinnamon to meat mixture. Stir in parsley. Add wine and cook until well blended and thick. Remove from stove. Add hard-cooked eggs; mix well. Stuff cheese with this mixture. Top with the cheese slice. Add a little water to flour to make a paste; seal cheese slice with flour paste and cover the cheese with oiled parchment to make an airtight package. Place in the top of a double boiler and cook for about 25 minutes until cheese is soft. While cheese steams, make sauce.

SAUCE FOR QUESO RELLENO

1 small onion, minced
1 green pepper, seeded and minced
3 tablespoons oil
2 tomatoes, peeled and chopped
2 cups beef bouillon
Shortening
½ cup flour
Salt and pepper to taste

Brown onion and green pepper in the hot oil. Add tomatoes, then bouillon. Cook for about 5 minutes, or until blended. Strain. Wipe out skillet and, in the same pan, add a little shortening and stir in the flour. When flour starts to brown, stir in the bouillon mixture slowly. Add salt and pepper to taste. Cook over a very low flame until thickened, stirring constantly. Pour over the cheese.

Helpful to know: Cheese scraped from the inside of the cheese ball can be grated for use in other recipes.

HUEVOS DE LOS CHARROS
(Cowboy's Eggs)

8 servings

1½ pounds ground beef
½ cup shortening
 2 onions, minced, divided
½ teaspoon thyme
   Salt and pepper to taste
½ teaspoon marjoram
1½ tablespoons chili powder
¾ cup light cream

3 tomatoes
3 avocados, peeled, pitted
   and mashed
   Pinch of coriander
8 tortillas
   Oil for frying
16 eggs, fried
½ cup grated mild cheese

Brown the beef in a small amount of hot shortening; add half of the onion and the thyme. When meat is done and onion is softened, add the salt, pepper, marjoram, chili powder, and cream. Toast the tomatoes for about 1 minute over high heat, peel them, and chop them well. Mix the tomatoes with the avocados, coriander, and the other half of the onion to form a paste. Season to taste. Fry the tortillas in a small amount of oil until crisp and brown. Place some of the meat mixture on each tortilla; put a mound of the avocado mixture in the center. Place 2 fried eggs on each tortilla, 1 on either side of the avocado sauce. Top with cheese and serve at once.
Helpful to know: You can buy tortillas canned or frozen.

PESCADO EN JUGO DE NARANJA
(Fish in Orange Juice)

8 servings

 8 white fish fillets
   Salt and pepper to taste
   Juice of 2 limes
 2 tablespoons olive oil
1½ tablespoons minced scallions
 2 tomatoes, peeled and chopped
1½ tablespoons chopped green pepper

2 tablespoons olive oil
½ cup orange juice
4 tablespoons drained capers
2 oranges, sliced thinly,
   including peel
½ cup toasted, blanched,
   chopped almonds

Season fish with salt and pepper and marinate it in the lime juice for about 20 minutes. Oil baking pan with 2 tablespoons olive oil and place fish in pan. Top the fish with minced scallion, tomatoes and green pepper and drizzle over this 2 tablespoons olive oil. Place in a preheated 350° oven, and when the fish begins to brown (about 15 minutes after it is placed in the oven), add the orange juice. Cook another 15 or 20 minutes, or until fish flakes easily when pierced with a fork. Garnish with capers, orange slices and almonds.

FRIJOLES CON PLATANOS
(Beans with Bananas)

8 servings

3 slices bacon
1 onion, chopped
⅔ cup tomato purée
2 cups canned kidney beans

Salt and pepper to taste
3 small bananas, peeled and
   cut into round slices

Sauté bacon; remove from the pan and cut into small pieces. In the bacon fat, sauté the onion until transparent, add the tomato purée and simmer for a few seconds. Add the beans, the bacon, and the salt and pepper to taste. Heat through and toss quickly with the banana slices.

Helpful to know: Make this dish up to the point of heating and adding the banana slices. Let stand. Then finish just before serving.

MOLLETES DE CALABAZA
(Pumpkin Muffins)

16 to 20 muffins

1 pound cooked, mashed pumpkin (canned will do)
¾ cup warm milk
2 eggs, beaten
3 cups flour

2 teaspoons salt
2 tablespoons baking powder
1 teaspoon ground cloves
1 cup white raisins

Mix pumpkin with milk. Stir well and add the eggs. Sift dry ingredients. Add to pumpkin mixture, stir in raisins, and pour into oiled muffin tins, filling only halfway. Bake in preheated 425° oven for 30 minutes, or until nicely browned.

ENSALADA DE CALABACITAS
(Squash Salad)

8 servings

8 medium-size zucchini
1 clove garlic
½ teaspoon cider vinegar
1 small onion, minced
3 stalks celery, chopped
5 tablespoons French Dressing (page 87)

Salt and freshly ground
pepper to taste
Lettuce leaves
Mayonnaise

Cut squash into pieces about ½ inch thick and place in a saucepan with a small amount of salted water, the garlic and the vinegar. Cover and cook about 6 minutes, or until tender but not too soft. Drain; remove garlic. Chill zucchini. Add all other ingredients except the lettuce leaves and mayonnaise. Toss. Serve on lettuce leaves with mayonnaise on top.

QUESO DE ALMENDRAS
(Mexican Almond Cheese)

8 servings

1 pound blanched almonds
1½ teaspoons vanilla extract
2 egg whites
7 egg yolks, lightly beaten

1¾ cups sugar
Cinnamon
8 small eating apples

Grind the almonds well and mix with vanilla, egg whites and yolks to make a paste. Boil the sugar with 1 cup of water until it reaches the soft-ball stage (236° on candy thermometer). Remove from heat and combine with ground almond-egg paste. Cook this mixture over a very low flame, stirring constantly, until bottom of the pan can be seen in the wake of the spoon. Remove from the fire and beat into a paste. Line a 1-quart mold with waxed paper and pour in mixture. Let cool, remove from mold, remove the paper, and dust with ground cinnamon until cheese is covered completely. Cut into small wedges when serving and accompany with apples—or with pears, if preferred.

CHOCOLATE MEXICANO
(Mexican Chocolate)   8 servings

4 ounces Mexican *or*   6 cups milk
   semisweet American chocolate   1½ teaspoons cinnamon

Combine all and cook over a low flame, stirring constantly, until mixture is blended and all the chocolate has melted. Beat to a froth before serving. Serve hot in cups or mugs.

THE SOUL-FOOD WAY

Maybe if everyone were born rich, Soul Food would not be in existence. Maybe. But if that's the case, why do so many people go on eating —and relishing—Soul Food long after they can afford something "better"? Black people feel Soul Food is their own, but that's not necessarily so —some of its ways of cooking originated with the Indians, some with poor white Southerners. Some with traders, explorers, settlers of many national origins. Soul Food belongs to all of us—try it, and you'll see why. You'll have no trouble finding the ingredients for any of these recipes at any large supermarket. As for the pork rinds and the watermelon pickles, you can buy those—the first in bags like potato chips, the second in jars.

Smirnoff 'n' Ciders
Yam Chips   Pork Rinds
Kentucky Burgoo   Baked Grits and Cheese
Sausage and Rice
Southern Slaw   Pickled Watermelon Rind
Virginia Fried Peaches   Shortnin' Bread
Coffee

SMIRNOFF 'N' CIDER
                                                              1 drink
2 ounces Smirnoff Vodka   Apple cider

Put vodka into an 8-ounce glass. Add 2 cubes of ice. Fill with cider. Stir. Garnish with apple slice, if desired.

YAM CHIPS
8 servings

6 yams
Salt

Oil or shortening for
deep-fat frying

Peel yams and slice as thinly as you can—as if you were making potato chips. Soak for 3 hours in cold salted water. Drain well and pat dry with paper towels. Drop a few at a time in deep fat heated to 400° and cook until golden brown. Drain thoroughly. Sprinkle with salt while hot.

KENTUCKY BURGOO
8 to 10 servings

2 tablespoons bacon fat
1 pound lean shin bones of beef,
   with meat
1 pound shoulder of veal, cubed
1 chicken, 1¼ pounds
2 teaspoons salt
2 cups chopped onions
1 tablespoon bacon fat
1 clove garlic, minced
1 cup diced raw potatoes
5 stalks celery, diced
1 can (1 pound) tomatoes
3 carrots, pared and diced

1 green pepper, seeded and chopped
1 cup butter beans *or* limas
¼ teaspoon crushed red pepper
   or dash cayenne
2 cloves
1 bay leaf
1 tablespoon dark brown sugar
   Dash pepper
1 cup sliced okra
3 ears *or* 1 can (12 ounces) corn
¼ cup butter
½ cup flour
½ cup snipped parsley

Heat 2 tablespoons bacon fat in a dutch oven. Add beef bones and veal and brown well. Add chicken, 2 quarts of water and salt. Cover and cook over low heat until veal and chicken are tender. Remove from broth. When cool enough to handle, remove all skin and bones. Cut meat into bite-size pieces and return to broth. In a skillet, cook onions in 1 tablespoon bacon fat until pale golden. Add to broth with garlic, potatoes, celery, tomatoes, carrots, green pepper, butter beans, red pepper, cloves, bay leaf, brown sugar and pepper. Cook slowly about 1½ hours. Add okra and corn; cook 15 minutes. Blend butter and flour. Stir into burgoo until thickened. Correct seasoning. Sprinkle with parsley.
Helpful to know: Make this in advance, refrigerate it and heat it up to serve—it will be all the better.

BAKED GRITS AND CHEESE
8 servings

3 tablespoons butter
½ large onion, finely chopped
1 teaspoon salt
¾ cup hominy grits
1 teaspoon (or less, if you're
   timid) Tabasco sauce

Dash of black pepper
1½ cups grated Cheddar cheese
3 egg whites, stiffly beaten

Melt butter in skillet; sauté onion until pale golden. Bring 3 cups water to a boil. Add salt; slowly add grits, stirring. Reduce heat and cook 3 minutes. Add onion, Tabasco, pepper and about three-quarters of the cheese. Fold in egg whites. Place mixture in a lightly oiled 2½-quart casserole. Sprinkle with remaining cheese. Bake in a preheated 400° oven for about 30 minutes.

Helpful to know: Find hominy grits in the cereal department of your supermarket. This, too, can be made in advance, refrigerated and baked just before serving. If you refrigerate it, bake about 40 minutes.

SAUSAGE AND RICE
8 servings

1½ pounds bulk sausage
1 large onion, sliced
1¼ cups uncooked rice

1¼ cups diced celery
2 teaspoons salt
Dash black pepper

Roll sausage into small balls and cook in dutch oven until lightly browned on all sides, about 10 minutes. Remove and reserve. Pour off all but about 3 tablespoons fat. Add onion and rice and cook until golden. Add sausage, remaining ingredients and 1½ cups water. Bring to a boil. Cover, lower heat and simmer about 40 minutes, until liquid is absorbed, stirring occasionally.

Helpful to know: Cook about 20 minutes, refrigerate, cook again for 30 minutes just before serving.

SOUTHERN SLAW
8 servings

1 large head cabbage
1½ cups chopped, cooked ham
1 green pepper, seeded and chopped
1 sweet red pepper, seeded and chopped

1 large onion, chopped
Salt and pepper to taste
1 egg white
1 cup (about) mayonnaise

Chop cabbage finely. Mix ham, peppers and onion and add to cabbage. Season to taste. Refrigerate until just before you are ready to serve. Beat the egg white until frothy, use to thin mayonnaise. Add to slaw and toss.

Try this way: If you like, a little vinegar and/or sugar may be added to the mayonnaise before dressing the slaw.

VIRGINIA FRIED PEACHES
8 servings

8 peaches
3 tablespoons butter

1 tablespoon dark brown sugar
Vanilla ice cream

Peel and split the peaches; remove the pits. Melt butter in a large skillet and put in the peaches, rounded side down. Fill the hollows with brown sugar. Simmer until just beginning to get soft. Serve with a spoonful of vanilla ice cream on top of each peach half.

SHORTNIN' BREAD

about 30 cookies

4 cups flour
1 cup light brown sugar,
   firmly packed

1 pound butter, melted

Mix flour and sugar. Add butter and mix well. Turn out on floured surface and pat gently to about a ½-inch thickness. Cut into desired shapes with knife—diamonds are easy—and bake in a preheated 325° oven for 20 to 25 minutes, or until done but not browned.

THE GREEK WAY

It would be hard to find a more hospitable people than the Greeks— as a matter of fact, one Greek word, *xenos*, means both "foreigner" and "guest." So if you invite friends to share a Greek-style meal with you, you'll simply be doing something quite natural in Greece. Copy the Greek manner of welcoming each guest: Present him with a glass of ouzo, and on the side some feta cheese, a few Calamata olives and a slice of crusty bread. If you have a visitor during the early morning or afternoon hours, a bowl of Glyko (sweet preserve), a spoon and glass of ice cold water is the ideal welcome. The guest tastes a teaspoon of Glyko and chases it down with a long sip of cold water.

Arrow Ouzo   Glyko
Dolmadakia   Taramasalata
Moussaka   Fassolia me Arni
Spanakopita   Crusty Bread
Greek Salad
Loukoumades   Kourambiedes
Coffee

DOLMADAKIA

8 servings

(Stuffed Grape Leaves)

1 medium-size onion, chopped finely
2 eggs
1 cup uncooked rice
1 pound ground hamburger
   Salt, pepper, paprika, dry mint leaves

One jar of California grapevine leaves (imported leaves are tougher and hence less palatable)
Few pats butter
3 fresh juicy lemons

111

Blend the onion, 1 egg, rice, hamburger and spices. Float the grapevine leaves in a large bowl of water to dilute the brine content. Snip the stem from each leaf as it is used. Place the leaf, underside up, and position a small dab of the hamburger mixture in one corner. Then roll the leaf over the hamburger, tucking in the sides and end as you roll. (If the leaves are loosely wrapped, the rice will unravel the leaves as it cooks and expands.) Place the tightly rolled grapevine leaf at one side of a medium-sized sauce-pan. Place the succeeding leaves closely against the first leaf. The entire batch will result in about 3 layers of leaves. Place a heavy dish or two face down on the leaves and then cover the leaves gently with cold water to the level of the dishes. Drop a few pats of butter over the top of the water. Heat until water boils, then reduce heat and simmer until rice is well cooked. In a bowl place 1 raw egg and the juice from the lemons. Beat the egg and lemon with a fork for about 100 strokes. Slowly pour the wa-ter from the saucepan into the bowl of egg-lemon juice. Then slowly pour the egg-lemon base over all the grapevine leaves in the saucepan which has been removed from the heat. Since the egg-lemon sauce will settle quickly, the leaves should be placed into the bowl one at a time, which will result in the bottom leaves being inverted to the top and vice versa. Let the leaves stand about 5 minutes. Serve hot or cold.

TARAMASALATA
(Caviar Spread)

2¼ cups

3 slices white bread, crusts trimmed
1 jar (8 ounces) red caviar
⅓ cup finely chopped onion
¼ cup lemon juice

¾ cup olive oil
Thinly sliced crusty white-bread chunks

Soak the bread in 1 cup water for 5 minutes; squeeze out all the water and mash bread until smooth. Add caviar, onion and lemon juice; mix until smooth. Mix in olive oil very gradually until mixture is pale pink. Chill. Serve with crusty white-bread chunks.

GREEK MOUSSAKA
(Ground Meat with Eggplant)

8 to 10 servings

3 medium-size eggplants
1 cup butter, divided
3 large onions, finely chopped
2 pounds ground lamb *or* beef
3 tablespoons tomato paste
½ cup red wine
½ cup snipped parsley
¼ teaspoon cinnamon
Salt to taste

Freshly ground black pepper to taste
6 tablespoons flour
1 quart milk
4 eggs, beaten until frothy
Nutmeg
2 cups ricotta *or* cottage cheese
1 cup fine, dry bread crumbs
1 cup freshly grated Parmesan cheese

Peel the eggplants and cut them into slices about ½ inch thick. Brown the slices quickly in ¼ cup butter. Set aside. Heat ¼ cup butter in the same skillet and cook the onions until they are browned. Add the ground meat and cook 10 minutes. Combine the tomato paste with the wine, parsley, cinnamon, salt and pepper. Stir this mixture into the meat and simmer over low heat, stirring frequently, until all the liquid has been absorbed. Remove the mixture from the heat. Make a white sauce by melting ½ cup butter and blending in the flour, stirring with a wire whisk. Meanwhile, bring the milk to a boil and add it gradually to the butter-flour mixture, stirring constantly. When the mixture is thickened and smooth, remove it from the heat. Cool slightly and stir in the beaten eggs, nutmeg and ricotta cheese. Oil an 11- x 14-inch pan and sprinkle the bottom lightly with bread crumbs. Arrange alternate layers of eggplant and meat sauce in the pan, sprinkling each layer with Parmesan cheese and bread crumbs. Pour the ricotta cheese sauce over the top and bake in a preheated 375° oven for 1 hour, or until top is golden. Remove from the oven and cool 20 to 30 minutes before serving. Cut into squares and serve.

Helpful to know: The flavor of this dish improves on standing one day. Reheat before serving.

FASSOLIA ME ARNI
(Bean-Lamb Casserole)

8 to 10 servings

3 cups dried white beans	¾ teaspoon black pepper
3 tablespoons olive oil	1½ bay leaves
2 cups chopped onions	2¼ cups peeled, chopped tomatoes
1 piece boneless lamb, about 3 pounds, cubed	3 cloves garlic, minced
1 tablespoon salt	3 tablespoons finely snipped parsley

Wash the beans, cover with water and bring to a boil. Cook 5 minutes, remove from heat and let stand 1 hour. Drain. Add fresh water, cover, bring to a boil and simmer over low heat for 1½ hours. Drain. Heat the oil in a flameproof casserole; brown the onions in it. Add lamb and cook until browned. Add beans, 1¾ cups boiling water, salt, pepper, bay leaves. Cover and cook over low heat 1 hour. Add tomatoes and garlic; re-cover and cook 1 hour longer, or until beans and lamb are tender. Sprinkle with parsley.

Helpful to know: This dish also improves on standing. Make the day before; heat in the oven to serve.

SPANAKOPITA
(Spinach Pie)

8 servings

2 pounds raw spinach	2 tablespoons minced fresh dillweed
2 teaspoons salt	2 tablespoons finely snipped parsley
¼ teaspoon pepper	½ pound feta (Greek) cheese, mashed
¾ cup olive oil, divided	¼ teaspoon pepper
1 cup chopped scallions	10 sheets phyllo pastry

Wash the spinach, drain and chop it. Sprinkle with the salt and ¼ teaspoon pepper. Let stand 1 hour. Drain thoroughly. Heat ¼ cup olive oil in a skillet; sauté the scallions 5 minutes. Mix in the spinach and cook over low heat 5 minutes, stirring frequently. Turn into a bowl; add dill, parsley, cheese and remaining pepper. Brush an 8- x 12-inch baking pan with oil. Line with 1 sheet of pastry. Brush with oil and cover with 4 more sheets, brushing each with oil. Spread the spinach mixture over the pastry and cover with remaining 5 sheets, brushing each with oil. Score the top into squares and brush lightly with cold water. Bake in a preheated 350° oven for 40 minutes, or until browned. Cool 10 minutes; cut into squares.

Helpful to know: Buy phyllo pastry in Greek, Armenian or Turkish stores or in gourmet shops—or use packaged strudel leaves.

GREEK SALAD
8 servings

1½ quarts torn salad greens, washed and drained	Lemon juice
2 cucumbers, peeled and sliced	8 small radishes, cleaned
6 scallions, chopped	3 tomatoes, quartered
Salt and pepper to taste	16 anchovy fillets
Olive oil	16 pitted ripe olives
	½ pound feta cheese, crumbled

Place salad greens in a bowl and mix in cucumbers and scallions. Season. Dress with combined oil and lemon juice in proportions to suit your taste, using just enough to coat greens nicely. Arrange remaining ingredients attractively on top. Just before serving, toss to incorporate all ingredients.

LOUKOUMADES
(Sesame Honey Puffs)
8 servings

2 cups plain yogurt	1 teaspoon baking soda
½ teaspoon grated orange peel	3 cups flour
½ teaspoon cinnamon	Oil or shortening for deep-fat frying
⅛ teaspoon ground cloves	Cinnamon Honey Syrup
1 teaspoon salt	2 tablespoons sesame seeds, toasted
¼ cup brandy	

Combine yogurt, orange peel, cinnamon, cloves and salt in a large bowl. Blend brandy and baking soda; add to yogurt mixture. Gradually beat in flour to form a smooth dough. Cover and set aside 2 hours. Drop by tablespoonfuls in deep hot oil. Fry until golden brown (about 6 minutes), turning once. Drain puffs on paper towels; layer in large brandy snifter or crystal bowl (make sure that serving bowl will stand heat of syrup). Pour hot Cinnamon Honey Syrup over each layer of puffs; sprinkle with sesame seeds after each soaking with syrup. To serve, allow 2 puffs per person; spoon excess Cinnamon Honey Syrup over each serving. Serve warm.

CINNAMON HONEY SYRUP

1½ cups

1½ cups honey	1 tablespoon lemon juice
½ teaspoon ground cinnamon	1 tablespoon brandy

Combine honey, ⅓ cup water and cinnamon in a small saucepan. Boil 5 minutes; turn heat down to simmer until ready to pour over puffs. Just before pouring, blend in lemon juice and brandy.

KOURAMBIEDES
(Greek Clove Cookies)

65 to 70 cookies

½ pound sweet butter	2½ cups sifted flour
½ cup confectioners sugar	Whole cloves
½ yolk of an egg	Confectioners sugar for coating
1½ tablespoons brandy *or* whiskey	

Soften the butter at room temperature. Cream it well, gradually add the confectioners sugar and beat until light and fluffy. This may be done in an electric mixer. Add the ½ egg yolk and the brandy or whiskey and beat at medium-high speed until the mixture is very pale in color. Add the flour gradually, blending it into the mixture on very low speed or with a wooden spoon. Chill the dough about 20 minutes to facilitate handling, and shape it into 1½-inch crescents or half-moons or small balls. Stud each cookie with a whole clove inserted up to the bud end. Bake on unoiled cookie sheets in a preheated 325° oven for 25 to 30 minutes, or until light brown. Sift confectioners sugar onto waxed paper. Place the warm *kourambiedes* on the sugar and sift more sugar over the cookies. Toss lightly until well coated. Cool on wire racks.

THE ITALIAN WAY

Choose a not-quite-spring day to invite friends to share this savory brunch—even in the gloomiest weather, it can almost make you feel that unbelievable Mediterranean sun. Italians' love of life and love of good food go hand in hand. You can play up the theme by dressing your table in Italy's red-white-green colors—a green tablecloth, for instance, with dishes of white ironstone and bouquets of red carnations blessing the room with their clovelike, won't-fight-with-food scent.

Smirnoff and Tonics (page 66)
Antipasto
Vitello Tonnato   Fettucine Alfredo
Melanzane Gratinate   Italian Bread
Insalata Siciliana
Torta Ricotta   Coffee

ANTIPASTO
(Assorted Appetizers)

- 1 head romaine lettuce
- 2 jars (5 ounces each) marinated artichoke hearts
- 16 slices salami
- Pickled mushrooms (page 62)
- 16 scallions, cleaned and trimmed
- 16 stalks celery, cleaned and trimmed
- 8 hard-cooked eggs, page 137, shelled and sliced
- 16 tomato wedges

- 16 anchovy fillets
- 2 jars (4 ounces each) pimientos, drained
- 2 stalks finocchio, quartered
- Ripe olives (Italian style, preferably)
- 8 rings green pepper
- 8 slices prosciutto
- Olive oil
- Red wine vinegar
- Salt and pepper to taste

Place several leaves of romaine on each of 8 salad plates. Divide remaining ingredients except Italian ham—prosciutto—among the plates, placing in an attractive pattern and topping with a slice of prosciutto. Have on the table oil and vinegar in cruets and mills of salt and black pepper so that each guest may dress his own antipasto as he chooses.
Idea: Place all antipasto ingredients on a large serving plate, if desired.

VITELLO TONNATO
(Veal in Tuna-Fish Sauce)

8 to 12 servings

- 1 rolled leg of veal, 7 pounds
- 1 tablespoon salt
- ¼ teaspoon freshly ground black pepper
- 2 tablespoons olive oil
- 1 cup sliced onion
- 2 carrots, pared and sliced
- 6 sprigs parsley

- 2 cloves garlic
- 2 cloves
- 2 cans (7 ounces each) tuna, drained
- 12 anchovy fillets
- ½ cup lemon juice
- 1½ cups olive oil
- 4 teaspoons drained capers

Rub the veal with the salt and pepper. Brown the veal in 2 tablespoons olive oil over high heat in a dutch oven or heavy saucepan. Pour off the fat. Add the onion, carrots, parsley, garlic, cloves and 7 cups boiling water. Cover and cook over low heat for 2 hours, or until veal is tender. Drain, dry and cool. Slice the veal and arrange in a glass or pottery bowl. Purée the tuna, anchovies and lemon juice in covered container of electric blender set at medium speed or force through a food mill. Very gradually beat in the oil. The sauce should look like thin mayonnaise. Mix in the capers. Pour the sauce over the veal. Marinate in the refrigerator 24 hours before serving.

FETTUCINE ALFREDO
(Egg Noodles with Butter and Cheese)

8 servings

- 2 pounds fettucine *or* broad egg noodles
- ½ pound (2 sticks) butter

- 2 cups freshly grated Parmesan cheese

Cook the noodles in boiling salted water until tender but still firm. Drain. Cut the butter into small pieces and put in a deep, heated serving dish. Add the fettucine and sprinkle with the cheese. Using a fork and spoon, quickly and lightly toss the fettucine until well coated with the butter and cheese.

MELANZANE GRATINATE
(Baked Eggplant with Cheese)

8 servings

¼ cup fine, dry bread crumbs
½ cup sifted flour
1 teaspoon salt
2 medium-size eggplants, peeled and sliced
1 cup milk

½ cup butter, divided
2 eggs, beaten
¾ pound mozzarella cheese, grated
3 tablespoons grated Parmesan cheese

Combine bread crumbs, flour and salt on a piece of waxed paper or in a wide, shallow dish. Dip eggplant slices in milk, then in crumb mixture, coating well. Melt half the butter in a skillet. Sauté the eggplant until browned on both sides, adding more butter if necessary. Combine eggs and the two cheeses; arrange half the eggplant on the bottom of a 9½- x 13- x 2-inch baking dish. Spread cheese mixture over it; top with remaining eggplant. Bake in a preheated 375° oven for 20 minutes.
Helpful to know: Prepare this the day before, if you like, and refrigerate. In that case, bake 30 minutes.

INSALATA SICILIANA
(White-Bean Salad)

8 servings

2 cans (20 ounces each) cannolini (Italian white beans)
2 large Italian red onions, chopped
1½ cups chopped celery
¾ cup sliced, stuffed olives

Salt and pepper to taste
½ cup olive oil
3 tablespoons white wine vinegar
Snipped parsley

Drain beans; mix with onions, celery and olives. Season well. Combine oil and vinegar. Pour just enough over salad to coat the ingredients well. Refrigerate overnight. Remove from refrigerator an hour before serving. Sprinkle with parsley.

TORTA RICOTTA
(Cheese Layer Cake)

8 servings

¾ pound ricotta
½ cup superfine sugar
3 egg yolks
3 tablespoons Arrow Curaçao
4 tablespoons finely grated unsweetened chocolate

1 8-inch round sponge cake
2 tablespoons Arrow Curaçao
1 cup heavy cream
Cinnamon

Beat the cheese and sugar until light, then beat in the egg yolks until fluffy. Remove half the mixture, and mix into the remaining half 3 table-spoons curaçao and the chocolate. Split the sponge cake in half, making 2 layers. Place 1 layer in a deep dish. Mix the remaining curaçao with ¼ cup water and pour over the layer. Spread the plain cheese mixture on it, then the chocolate mixture. Cover with the remaining sponge layer. Chill several hours. Whip the cream and spread it over the cake. Sprinkle with a little cinnamon.

BRUNCH IT YOURSELF

Here are more good-for-brunch dishes—around which you can build your own, suit-yourself brunch menus.

SMIRNOFF MULE
1 drink

1½ ounces Smirnoff Vodka   Stick of cucumber
   Ginger beer

In a special brass or copper mug, or in a highball glass, put a cube of ice and the vodka. Fill the glass with ginger beer and garnish with the stick of cucumber.

SMIRNOFF SPLENDID
1 drink

1½ ounces Smirnoff Vodka   Strip of lemon peel
 ½ ounce Arrow Anisette

Place vodka, anisette and cracked ice in shaker; shake until blended and chilled. Strain into cocktail glass. Decorate with lemon peel.

EGGS CZARINA
6 servings

3 tablespoons melted butter	½ cup dry white wine
2 tablespoons black caviar	1¼ cups dairy sour cream, scalded
6 eggs	Salt and pepper to taste
1½ tablespoons butter	Lemon juice (optional)
2 small white onions, finely chopped	

Brush 6 individual custard cups with melted butter; drop a teaspoon of caviar into each cup. Break an egg into each cup. Melt butter in saucepan; cook onion in butter until soft but not browned, stirring constantly. Add wine; stir and cook over low heat until liquid evaporates. Stir in sour cream and cook 5 minutes, stirring from bottom of saucepan. Strain and season to taste. Add a few drops of lemon juice if desired. Cover egg in each cup with 2 to 3 tablespoons sauce. Place cups on baking sheet. Bake in a pre-heated 325° oven for 15 minutes. Serve at once, in cups.

NEAPOLITAN EGG PIE

4 servings

Plain pastry for one 9-inch
pie crust
4 eggs
¼ cup milk
1 cup flaked, cooked white fish

½ pound mozzarella cheese, grated
¼ teaspoon salt
¼ teaspoon pepper
½ teaspoon basil
½ teaspoon oregano

Line a 9-inch pie plate with pastry. Beat eggs and milk together until well blended. Add remaining ingredients; stir well. Spoon into unbaked pie crust. Bake in a preheated 425° oven until browned, 30 to 35 minutes. Cut into wedges. Serve hot.

DANISH FRIED EGGS

6 servings

6 slices white bread
1 can (2½ to 3 ounces) deviled ham
⅓ cup butter

6 eggs
Parsley sprigs

Cut six 3-inch circles from bread with cookie cutter and reserve for another use. Spread bread slices with deviled ham. Melt butter in skillet and sauté bread until brown. Drop an egg in center of each. Cover and cook until bread is crisp and egg is set. Garnish with parsley sprigs.

WEST INDIAN SCRAMBLED EGGS

9 servings

1½ cups tomato sauce
¼ cup minced scallions
   or green pepper
2 tablespoons flour
⅔ cup grated white Cheddar cheese
2 medium-size avocados

12 eggs
⅔ cup light cream
Butter
Salt to taste
Grated white Cheddar cheese

Combine tomato sauce with scallions or green pepper and flour in a saucepan. Stir to blend. Bring to a boil and cook, stirring, 2 to 3 minutes. Add grated cheese and stir to combine. Remove from heat. Cut avocados in halves lengthwise; remove seed and skin and cut fruit into cubes. Add to tomato sauce. *Do not cook.* Beat eggs with cream in a bowl and scramble in butter in saucepan. Season and arrange on serving plate. Pour tomato and avocado sauce over eggs. Sprinkle top with grated Cheddar cheese.

EGGS, TOLEDO STYLE

6 servings

1 cup chopped, cooked ham
1 tablespoon olive oil
2 cups cooked peas
2 canned pimientos, chopped

¼ cup chopped, stuffed olives
Salt and pepper to taste (optional)
6 eggs
2 tablespoons olive oil

Sauté ham in olive oil for 2 or 3 minutes; then combine with peas, pimientos and olives. Heat well and add salt and pepper, if necessary. Place in the center of a hot platter and surround with eggs fried in olive oil.

BONUS: ALL ABOUT MAKING COFFEE

Start by buying the best brand of coffee—that is, the brand that makes the coffee which best suits your taste. Choose the proper grind for the coffee maker you prefer: regular for percolators, drip grind for drip pots, drip or fine grind for vacuum coffee makers. Using the right grind is important, for the coffee must be fine enough for the water to circulate freely and extract all the good coffee flavor, but not so fine that the brewed coffee will be cloudy and leave a muddy sediment in the cup.

Be sure that your coffee maker is always completely clean—after each use, wash all parts of it in hot water, using a good detergent and, if necessary, a brush to clean the spout and other small parts. Rinse thoroughly—many a bad cup of coffee tastes that way because there were traces of soap or detergent in the pot. Before each use, rinse pot with hot water.

Use your coffee maker to at least three-quarters of its capacity; you can't hope to make two cups of good, rich-tasting, satisfying coffee in an eight-cup maker. Coffee should always be fresh—don't buy more than you will use in a week. Keep the container tightly closed and stored in a cool, dry place—the refrigerator is ideal. For each serving (cup) of coffee, use 2 level tablespoons coffee and ¾ cup (6 fluid ounces) water. Don't skimp—coffee can't be stretched. Always use fresh cold water.

Coffee is at its best when it is freshly prepared. Always serve it piping hot and as soon as it is ready, if possible. If you must keep the coffee standing for a time, place the pot—unless it is an electric one—in a pan of water over a *very* low flame. Make certain that it doesn't boil.

Percolator: Measure fresh cold water into the bottom of the pot and regular-grind coffee, in the proper proportion, into the basket. The water level should always be below the bottom of the basket. Put the basket in place in the pot, cover, heat until water starts to bubble into the top. Reduce heat. When the water becomes amber-colored, start timing; let the coffee percolate gently 6 to 8 minutes. Remove basket.

Drip Pot: Measure drip-grind coffee into the filter (middle) section and put it and the upper section into place. Measure freshly boiled water into the upper section and cover. When all the water has dripped through the ground coffee into the lower section of the pot, remove upper and filter sections. Stir coffee and serve.

Vacuum Coffee Maker: Measure fresh cold water into the lower bowl and place over heat. Put filter into upper bowl, and measure in fine- or drip-grind coffee. When water boils, insert upper bowl, giving it a slight twist to make sure of a tight seal. The water—most of it—will rise into the upper bowl. When it has done so, reduce heat, stir thoroughly and let the brew bubble gently 2 minutes. Remove from heat. In no more than 3 minutes the brewed coffee will have returned to the lower bowl. Remove the upper part and serve the coffee.

THE OPEN-HOUSE BRUNCH

"FOR A JOB WELL DONE, THANK YOU"

The fund-raising drive is over, and it was a big success. Now, how do you say thank you to all the people who worked so hard? Simple—have a brunch for all the willing workers. Not only will they have a good time but, come next year, they'll all be on your committee again!

Smirnoff Mint Sparkle
Barbecue Dip   Raw Vegetables   Cocktail Franks
Liver-Pâté Appetizers   Ham Clouds
Stamp-and-Go Fritters
Barbecued Chicken-Little Wings   Dressy Deviled Eggs
Fresh Fruit   Cheese Board
Coffee

SMIRNOFF MINT SPARKLE
10 to 12 drinks

⅓ cup Arrow Green Crème de Menthe
2 cans (12 ounces each) unsweetened pineapple juice
½ cup lemon juice
1 cup Smirnoff Vodka
1 bottle (1 pint, 12 ounces) ginger ale, chilled

Combine crème de menthe and 1½ cups water in a punch bowl. Add pineapple juice and lemon juice and chill. Stir in vodka. Add a large block of ice. Add ginger ale.

BARBECUE DIP
1⅓ cups

½ cup chili sauce
⅔ cup dairy sour cream
1 teaspoon horseradish
2 teaspoons Worcestershire sauce
1 teaspoon lemon juice
Dash of Tabasco sauce
Heated cocktail franks
Fresh raw vegetables

In a small bowl combine all ingredients except franks and vegetables and blend well. Chill until ready to serve. Serve with heated cocktail franks and fresh raw vegetables.

LIVER-PATE APPETIZERS

32 appetizers

1 package refrigerated crescent
 rolls
2 cans (4¾ ounces each)
 liverwurst spread

5 slices crisply cooked bacon,
 drained and crumbled
¼ cup thinly sliced scallions

Separate roll dough at perforations. Generously cover each large triangle
with liverwurst spread. Cut each triangle into 4 small triangles. Sprinkle
bacon and onion over liverwurst. Roll each triangle up or leave flat, if desired. On baking sheet, bake in a preheated 375° oven for 10 minutes.

HAM CLOUDS

45 appetizers

1 can (4½ ounces) deviled ham
¼ cup bottled Thousand Island
 dressing
1 package (8 ounces) cream cheese,
 at room temperature
1 egg yolk

1 teaspoon baking powder
 Dash of salt
10 to 12 slices firm-textured white
 sandwich bread
 Paprika

In a small bowl mix deviled ham with Thousand Island dressing. In medium-size bowl, combine cream cheese with egg yolk, baking powder and
salt; mix until blended and smooth. Using a biscuit cutter about 1¼ inches
in diameter, cut 4 rounds from each slice of bread. Spread each round
with a layer of ham mixture. Spoon about 1 teaspoon of the cheese mixture on the ham. Sprinkle with paprika and bake in a preheated 375° oven
for 12 to 15 minutes, or until puffed and lightly browned.

STAMP-AND-GO FRITTERS

4 dozens

1 package (4 ounces) shredded
 salt codfish
½ cup sifted flour
½ teaspoon baking powder
¾ teaspoon thyme
⅛ teaspoon ground red pepper

1 teaspoon minced onion
⅓ cup finely chopped fresh tomato
2 teaspoons lime juice
 Oil or shortening for
 deep-fat frying

Prepare codfish as directed on package and set aside. Sift together flour,
baking powder, thyme and red pepper. Blend in onion. Add tomato, lime
juice, ½ cup cold water and codfish. Mix well. Drop from a teaspoon into
deep oil heated to 370° and fry until crisp and brown. (These should be
very crisp.) Serve piping hot on toothpicks.

BARBECUED CHICKEN-LITTLE WINGS

28 pieces

3 pounds chicken wings
½ cup salad oil
½ cup lemon juice
1 clove garlic, crushed

1 teaspoon salt
⅛ teaspoon pepper
½ cup chopped, stuffed olives

Cut chicken wings apart at both joints; reserve tips for soup stock. Combine disjointed wing pieces with remaining ingredients in a large bowl. Marinate several hours or overnight in the refrigerator, turning occasionally. Arrange wing pieces on a rack in a shallow roasting pan. Roast in a preheated 450° oven for 35 to 45 minutes, or until crisp and brown. Spoon marinade over wings several times during roasting period.

DRESSY DEVILED EGGS

24 egg halves

12 hard-cooked eggs (page 137), shelled
½ cup bottled Thousand Island dressing

2 tablespoons snipped chives
Salt and pepper to taste
Caviar, anchovy strips or chopped salted almonds

Cut eggs in half lengthwise and remove yolks. In a small bowl mash yolks with Thousand Island dressing. Add chives, salt and pepper. Press egg yolk mixture through a pastry tube into whites. Top each filled egg with ¼ teaspoon caviar, an anchovy strip or chopped almonds.

POLITICAL RALLY

Your favorite candidate is coming to town on his political swing, and it's your job to see that he meets the people. The best way for him to meet the most people is with a brunch, at your house, maybe even a staggered brunch with people coming in shifts. You'll be having a mob, so a punch-and-finger-foods party is in order. It can all be prepared and ready in advance, giving you time to aid your candidate in his quest for votes.

Smirnoff Election Punch
Shrimp-Cucumber Dip
Stuffed Mushrooms   Crispy Chicken Nuggets
Sherried Chicken-Liver Spread
Sharp Snacks   Cheese-Sausage Rolls
Roquefort Meatballs
Almond Tarts   Coffee

SMIRNOFF ELECTION PUNCH

24 drinks

2 quarts cranberry juice
1 can (6 ounces) frozen orange juice concentrate, undiluted, thawed
¼ cup sugar

1 pint Smirnoff Vodka
2 bottles (7 ounces each) carbonated water

Combine cranberry juice, orange juice and sugar in a punch bowl and stir until sugar is dissolved. Stir in vodka. Add a large block of ice. Carefully pour carbonated water over punch. Garnish with lemon and orange slices if desired.

SHRIMP-CUCUMBER DIP
2 cups

1 medium-size cucumber, unpared
1 cup creamy cottage cheese
2 tablespoons minced onion
2 teaspoons white vinegar

½ teaspoon horseradish
1 can (4½ ounces) shrimp, drained and chopped
Crisp crackers *or* vegetable sticks

Cut cucumber in half lengthwise; remove seeds and discard. Shred enough cucumber to make 1 cup. Drain well. Combine shredded cucumber, cottage cheese, onion, vinegar and horseradish. Beat until smooth. Fold in shrimp. Serve with crisp crackers or vegetable sticks.

STUFFED MUSHROOMS
24 mushrooms

24 large mushrooms
2 packages (3 ounces each) cream cheese, at room temperature
2 cans (4½ ounces each) deviled ham

¼ cup minced green pepper
2 tablespoons minced onion
¼ teaspoon finely crushed marjoram
Parsley sprigs

Remove stems carefully from mushrooms and reserve for some other use. Wipe caps with damp paper towel. Place mushroom caps, rounded side down, on a shallow tray. Blend remaining ingredients except parsley. Fill caps with mixture. Cover and chill. When ready to serve, top each with a small sprig of parsley.

CRISPY CHICKEN NUGGETS
2 to 3 dozens

2 whole broiler-fryer chicken breasts
¼ cup butter, melted
½ cup packaged corn-flake crumbs *or* seasoned bread crumbs

1 teaspoon salt
¼ teaspoon pepper

Bone chicken breasts; remove skin. Cut each breast half into 6 or 8 chunks, about 1½ inches square. Dip chicken in melted butter. Roll in crumbs combined with salt and pepper. Place in single layer in a shallow baking pan. Bake in a preheated 400° oven for 10 minutes. Serve hot or cold, with toothpicks.

SHERRIED CHICKEN-LIVER SPREAD
12 servings

1½ pounds chicken livers
1½ teaspoons anchovy paste
6 strips crisply cooked bacon, crumbled
1 tablespoon grated onion
2 tablespoons finely snipped parsley
¼ teaspoon pepper

⅓ cup minced pistachio nuts *or* blanched almonds
½ teaspoon dried oregano
¾ teaspoon dried basil
3 tablespoons butter, melted
3 tablespoons dry sherry
Crisp crackers *or* rye-bread rounds

Simmer livers in a small amount of boiling salted water until tender. Drain well. Place half of the livers in blender container with anchovy paste, bacon, onion, parsley and pepper. Cover and blend until smooth. Blend remaining livers with remaining ingredients except crackers. Combine mixtures. Pack into a mold and chill several hours or overnight. Serve with crisp crackers or rounds of rye bread.

SHARP SNACKS
30 snacks

1 package (6 ounces) sharp Cheddar cheese
¼ cup butter

½ cup flour
Pinch of salt
Dash cayenne

Mix all ingredients and blend with a pastry blender until the consistency of cornmeal. Roll into balls about ½ inch in diameter. Chill. Place on a baking sheet and bake in a preheated 400° oven for 12 to 15 minutes. Serve immediately.

Helpful to know: To freeze, spread balls on a baking sheet and freeze. Pack in freezer bags. At serving time, remove number desired. Place on baking sheet and bake in a preheated 400° oven for 12 to 15 minutes. Serve immediately.

CHEESE-SAUSAGE ROLLS
50 to 60 servings

16 sausage links
16 slices thin-sliced white bread

1 cup shredded Cheddar cheese
¼ cup butter

Cook sausage links until done. Drain on paper towels. Cut crusts from bread. Combine cheese and butter. Spread on both sides of bread. Roll a sausage in each slice and fasten with wooden picks. Bake on an oiled baking sheet in a preheated 400° oven for 10 to 12 minutes. Slice each roll into 3 or 4 slices and serve piping hot.

ROQUEFORT MEATBALLS
60 meatballs

1½ pounds ground beef chuck
1 package (3 ounces) Roquefort cheese, crumbled
¾ teaspoon salt

⅛ teaspoon pepper
¼ cup butter
½ cup dry red wine

Combine beef, cheese, salt and pepper and blend well. Shape into tiny balls using 1 heaping teaspoon of meat for each ball. Melt butter in a skillet. Brown meatballs in hot butter, turning as needed to brown on all sides. Add wine; cover and cook slowly about 5 minutes, or until done. Serve from a chafing dish with toothpicks.

ALMOND TARTS

½ cup blanched almonds, chopped very finely
½ cup sugar
2 cups flour
¾ cup butter

1 egg, slightly beaten
¼ teaspoon almond extract
Fruit preserve
Heavy cream, whipped

Combine almonds, sugar and flour in mixing bowl. Cut in butter until particles are very fine. Add egg and almond extract. Gather mixture into ball, wrap in waxed paper and chill 1 hour. Working with one-fourth of dough at a time, pinch off pieces the size of walnuts. Dip thumb in flour and press dough evenly into tiny fluted molds. Put molds on baking sheet and bake in a preheated 325° oven for 12 minutes, or until golden. Let stand 2 minutes, then turn molds upside down on baking sheet and tap gently on bottoms to loosen. Cool and store airtight in cool place. When ready to serve, fill with fruit preserve folded into whipped cream.

"IT'S A HOUSEWARMING" BRUNCH

Come and see our new house . . . or apartment . . . or penthouse. A housewarming given in the middle of the day gives the guests a chance to wander around outside and admire the lawn, trees and flowers. Or maybe you want to show off your view from the twentieth floor. No matter what the scene, it can be fun—and also easy on the hostess. Lots of punch in a big bowl, a few cold things from the refrigerator and one or two hot items, all precooked and kept hot in your brand new chafing dishes. Come —eat, drink and admire our new pad.

Smirnoff Cup
Shrimp Seviche
Olive—Chicken—Liver Pâté   *Chestnut Meatballs*
Sautéed Chicken Chunks   *Assorted Crackers*
Tuna Spread
Gold-and-Emerald Ribbon Sandwiches
Fresh Fruit Bowl   *Coffee*

SMIRNOFF CUP

about 50 drinks

3 cups diced, fresh pineapple
1 quart fresh strawberries, washed, hulled and sliced
¾ pound confectioners sugar
2 cups Don Q Gold Rum

2 cups lemon juice
1½ cups orange juice
¾ cup grenadine
2 fifths Smirnoff Vodka
2 quarts ginger ale

Place fruit in punch bowl. Sprinkle sugar over fruit; add rum. Cover and let stand 4 hours or overnight. Add lemon juice, orange juice, grenadine and vodka. Add a block of ice. Stir to blend and chill. Add ginger ale and stir.

SHRIMP SEVICHE

8 to 12 servings

4 cups raw shrimp
1 cup finely chopped onion
½ cup finely chopped canned green
   chili peppers

1 teaspoon salt
Fresh lime juice
2 to 4 tablespoons olive oil

Remove veins from shrimp and split in halves lengthwise. Place in a glass dish with onion, chili peppers and salt. Add enough lime juice to completely cover shrimp. Cover tightly and refrigerate at least 6 hours. Toss shrimp occasionally during this time. To serve, drain and toss with olive oil.

OLIVE−CHICKEN-LIVER PATE

5 cups

¼ cup chopped shallots
¾ cup butter
2 pounds chicken livers
⅓ cup Madeira
½ teaspoon salt
⅛ teaspoon nutmeg
⅛ teaspoon pepper

Pinch of thyme
½ cup heavy cream
½ cup butter
¾ cup chopped, stuffed olives
Sliced stuffed olives or
parsley sprigs

In a large skillet sauté shallots in ¾ cup of the butter until tender but not browned. Remove with a slotted spoon and set aside. In the same skillet, sauté chicken livers, a few at a time, until lightly browned, using more of the butter if needed. Remove chicken livers. Pour Madeira into the skillet and add the seasonings. Bring mixture to a boil, stirring to loosen browned bits from bottom of skillet. Combine half the livers, shallots, Madeira and cream in blender container. Cover and process at medium speed until smooth. Repeat, blending remaining half. Melt remaining butter; blend into liver mixture with chopped olives. Turn into a 5-cup pâté mold or serving dish. Chill several hours or overnight. Garnish with olives or parsley.

CHESTNUT MEATBALLS

60 meatballs

2 cups soft bread crumbs
½ cup milk
1 tablespoon soy sauce
½ tablespoon garlic salt

¼ teaspoon onion powder
½ pound ground beef chuck
½ pound pork sausage meat
1 can (5 ounces) water chestnuts

Combine bread crumbs, milk, soy sauce, garlic salt, onion powder, chuck and sausage meat. Drain chestnuts and chop finely. Add to meat mixture and blend well. Form into 1-inch balls. Place meatballs on a large, shallow baking pan, such as a jelly-roll pan. Bake in a preheated 350° oven for 18 to 20 minutes, or until done. Serve from a chafing dish with toothpicks.

SAUTEED CHICKEN CHUNKS

2 to 3 dozens

2 whole broiler-fryer
   chicken breasts
6 tablespoons butter
½ teaspoon salt

¼ teaspoon garlic powder
¼ teaspoon thyme
1 tablespoon snipped parsley

Bone chicken breasts and remove skin. Cut each breast half into 6 or 8 chunks about 1½ inches square. Melt butter in a large skillet over high heat. Add chicken and sprinkle with salt, garlic powder and thyme. Cook 5 minutes, stirring constantly. To serve, turn into a chafing dish. Sprinkle with parsley. Serve with toothpicks.

TUNA SPREAD
3 cups

2 cans (7 ounces each) tuna, drained
2 packages (3 ounces each) cream cheese, at room temperature
2 teaspoons horseradish
½ teaspoon Worcestershire sauce
¼ cup finely chopped onion
1 clove garlic, minced
½ teaspoon celery salt
3 tablespoons mayonnaise
¼ teaspoon pepper
Assorted crackers

Flake tuna in a bowl. Add cream cheese and mix well. Add remaining ingredients except crackers, and blend. Refrigerate. Serve with crackers.

GOLD-AND-EMERALD RIBBON SANDWICHES
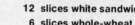
30 sandwiches

2 hard-cooked eggs (page 137), shelled
Mayonnaise
3 tablespoons chopped, raw spinach leaves
Pinch of salt
1 small ripe avocado
1 teaspoon lemon juice
12 slices white sandwich bread
6 slices whole-wheat bread

Mash eggs very well. Combine with ¼ cup mayonnaise, spinach leaves and salt. Peel avocado, pit and press through a sieve. Stir in lemon juice. Trim crust from white and whole-wheat bread slices. Spread white bread with mayonnaise. On 6 slices spread egg mixture. Spread whole-wheat bread with avocado mixture. Place avocado layer on top of egg layer. Top with remaining white slices, mayonnaise side down. Wrap in waxed paper and chill. Before serving, cut each sandwich into 5 ribbon slices.

BRUNCH IT YOURSELF

Here are more good-for-brunch dishes—around which you can build your own, suit-yourself brunch menus.

SMIRNOFF APPLE DANDY
1 drink

2 ounces Smirnoff Vodka   Canned apple juice, chilled

Place 2 ice cubes and vodka into an 8-ounce highball glass. Fill glass with apple juice and stir.

SMIRNOFF SPECIAL
1 drink

3 ounces Smirnoff Vodka
2 ounces beef bouillon
2 to 3 drops Tabasco sauce
2 dashes Worcestershire sauce
1 teaspoon lemon juice
Cocktail vegetable juice

Place 5 or 6 ice cubes in a 10-ounce glass. Add vodka, bouillon, Tabasco, Worcestershire and lemon juice. Fill glass with vegetable juice. Stir.

CHEDDAR-OLIVE BITES
40 appetizers

1 can (7½ ounces) extra-large, pitted ripe olives
Sharp Cheddar cheese
1 cup prepared biscuit mix

¼ teaspoon thyme
¼ teaspoon oregano
2 tablespoons melted butter
3 tablespoons milk

Drain olives. Cut cheese in small cubes and stuff olives with chunks of cheese. Combine biscuit mix and herbs. Stir in butter and milk to make a smooth dough. Mold a teaspoon of dough around each olive, covering it completely. Place on baking sheet. Bake in a preheated 400° oven for 10 to 12 minutes, or until lightly browned. Serve piping hot.

CHIPPED PARMESAN SWEETS
4 to 6 servings

2 pounds medium-size sweet potatoes
Oil or shortening for deep-fat frying

1 cup grated Parmesan cheese
Salt

Peel potatoes and cut into ¼-inch-thick slices. Heat oil in deep-fat fryer to 374°. Cook potatoes partially, or until just golden in color. Drain on absorbent paper. Just before serving, fry potatoes in hot oil for 1 minute, or enough to just brown. Drain on absorbent paper. Shake potatoes in Parmesan cheese and sprinkle with salt. Serve immediately.

ZIPPY BEEF-OLIVE SPREAD
1½ cups

1 teaspoon instant minced onion
1 tablespoon dry sherry
1 package (8 ounces) cream cheese, at room temperature
2 tablespoons mayonnaise

1 package (3 ounces) smoked sliced beef, finely snipped
¼ cup chopped, stuffed olives
Whole-wheat bread or unsalted crackers

Soften onion in sherry. Blend cream cheese with mayonnaise; add the sherry-onion mixture. Stir in beef and olives. Serve with triangles of whole-wheat bread or unsalted crackers.

HERB-CURRY DIP
1½ cups

1 cup mayonnaise
½ cup dairy sour cream
1 teaspoon crushed mixed herbs
¼ teaspoon salt
⅛ teaspoon curry powder

1 tablespoon snipped parsley
1 tablespoon grated onion
1½ teaspoons lemon juice
½ teaspoon Worcestershire sauce

Combine all ingredients. Blend well and chill before serving. Serve with carrot sticks, celery sticks and cauliflower buds.

HOT CRAB SPREAD

1¾ cups

1 package (8 ounces) cream cheese, at room temperature
1 tablespoon milk
2 teaspoons Worcestershire sauce
1 can (7½ ounces) crab meat, drained and flaked
2 tablespoons chopped green pepper
2 tablespoons toasted, slivered almonds
Assorted crackers

Combine cream cheese, milk and Worcestershire sauce. Add crab meat and pepper to cream-cheese mixture. Turn into a small shallow baking dish. Top with almonds. Bake in a preheated 350° oven for 15 minutes, or until heated through. Keep warm over candle warmer. Serve with crackers.

CHEESE BISCUITS

1 dozen

2 cups prepared biscuit mix
½ cup grated sharp Cheddar cheese
⅔ cup milk

Combine biscuit mix and cheese in a bowl. Stir in milk and blend lightly. Turn out onto lightly floured board; knead gently about 10 times. Pat out dough to ½-inch thickness and cut in rounds with a 2-inch biscuit cutter. Place on unoiled baking sheet. Bake in a preheated 450° oven for 10 to 15 minutes.

HOT CRAB-MEAT CANAPES

4 dozens

3 tablespoons butter
3 tablespoons flour
1 cup hot chicken broth
¼ cup light cream
Dash of pepper
1 teaspoon lemon juice
1 can (7 ounces) crab meat, drained and flaked
48 2-inch bread rounds, toasted
Grated Swiss cheese

Melt butter in a heavy saucepan. Stir in flour. Remove from heat and stir in broth and cream. Cook, stirring constantly, until mixture comes to a boil and thickens. Remove from heat. Blend in pepper, lemon juice and crab meat and mix well. Spread mixture on toasted bread rounds. Sprinkle with cheese. Arrange on a baking sheet and broil about 4 inches from source of heat for 2 to 3 minutes, or until lightly browned. Serve hot.

CHICKEN-AND-TONGUE SPREAD

3 cups

1 can (12 ounces) boned chicken, ground
1 jar (7 ounces) tongue, ground
1 small onion, grated
¼ teaspoon sage
¼ teaspoon thyme
½ cup dairy sour cream
Salt and pepper to taste
Melba toast or rye-bread rounds

Combine chicken, tongue, onion, sage, thyme and sour cream. Season to taste with salt and pepper. Chill 2 to 3 hours before serving. Serve with Melba toast or rounds of rye bread.

LIVERWURST LOG

3 cups

1 pound liverwurst
3 tablespoons dry sherry
1 tablespoon lemon juice
⅓ cup chopped sweet cucumber
    pickles
¾ cup chopped walnuts
2 teaspoons lemon juice
Gherkins
Crackers or rye-bread rounds

Mash liverwurst; add sherry and 1 tablespoon lemon juice; blend well. Reserve ½ cup liverwurst mixture. Combine remaining liverwurst mixture with chopped pickles and walnuts and mix well. Shape into a 10-inch roll. Combine reserved ½ cup liverwurst mixture and 2 teaspoons lemon juice and blend. Spread on top and sides of roll. Mark with a spatula to resemble a log. Chill at least 2 hours before serving. Garnish with gherkins before serving. Serve as a spread with crackers or rye-bread rounds.

CRUNCHY MUNCHY

12 servings

¼ cup butter
¼ cup salad oil
½ cup shelled walnuts or peanuts
1 cup ready-to-eat bite-size
    shredded rice
1 cup ready-to-eat bite-size
    shredded wheat
1 cup ready-to-eat
    doughnut-shaped cereal
1 cup thin pretzel sticks
1 teaspoon seasoned salt

Melt butter and mix with salad oil in a shallow baking pan. Place nuts, cereals and pretzels in pan. Toss very carefully with melted butter. Sprinkle salt over top. Bake in a preheated 300° oven for 30 minutes, stirring carefully with a wooden spoon every 10 minutes. Cool thoroughly.

HOT MUSHROOM CAPS

1 dozen

½ pound mushrooms
2 tablespoons melted butter
1 medium-size onion, finely
    chopped
2 tablespoons butter
½ cup chopped, stuffed olives
1 tablespoon dry sherry

Wash mushrooms, pat dry and carefully remove stems. Brush caps with 2 tablespoons butter. Place in a very shallow baking pan and broil, 4 inches from the source of the heat, about 5 minutes, or until lightly browned. Meanwhile chop mushroom stems. Cook stems and onion in 2 tablespoons butter in a skillet until lightly browned. Add olives and sherry. Mix well. Fill mushroom caps with olive mixture. Broil 3 to 4 inches from source of heat for 5 minutes, or until filling is lightly browned.

CLAMS CASINO

2 dozen cherrystone clams
  in the shells
½ cup finely chopped onion
½ cup finely chopped green pepper
1 clove garlic, crushed
¼ cup chopped pimiento
⅛ teaspoon Tabasco sauce

1 cup saltine cracker crumbs,
  divided
1 egg, beaten
¼ cup butter, melted
8 strips bacon, partially cooked
  and drained

Remove clams from shells; wash and save shells. Cook clams in boiling water for 10 minutes. Reserve a small amount of clam liquid. Drain and chop clams. Combine with onion, green pepper, garlic, pimiento, Tabasco and ¾ cup of the cracker crumbs. Stir in beaten egg, melted butter and enough of the reserved clam liquid to moisten well. Spoon lightly into clam shells. Sprinkle with remaining crumbs. Cut bacon into 1-inch pieces. Top each clam with a piece of bacon. Bake in a preheated 350° oven for 15 to 20 minutes. Serve piping hot.

CURRIED TURKEY SPREAD
1 cup

1 cup finely chopped, cooked turkey
¼ cup mayonnaise
1 tablespoon finely chopped
  chutney

1½ teaspoons curry powder

Combine ingredients and blend well. Chill. Serve with assorted crackers.

FROSTED HAM BALL
4½ cups

1 pound cooked ham, ground
½ cup dark seedless raisins
1 medium-size onion, grated
¾ cup mayonnaise
½ teaspoon curry powder

2 packages (3 ounces each) cream
  cheese, at room temperature
2 tablespoons milk
Snipped parsley
Assorted crackers and rye bread

Combine ham, raisins, onion, mayonnaise and curry powder. Blend well. Mold mixture into a ball on a serving plate. Chill. Blend cream cheese and milk. Frost ham mixture with cream-cheese mixture. Garnish with snipped parsley. Serve with assorted crackers and rye bread.

DIPSY DIP
1½ cups

¾ cup finely chopped bologna
½ cup chopped, pitted ripe olives
2 tablespoons chopped pimiento
2 tablespoons sweet pickle relish

¼ teaspoon garlic salt
Mayonnaise
Assorted crackers

Combine bologna, olives, pimiento, pickle relish and garlic salt. Stir in enough mayonnaise to make mixture of dip consistency. Cover and chill. Serve with assorted crackers.

BONUS: ALL ABOUT BUTTERS AND EGGS

Any one of these savory or sweet butters will dress up any bread you bring to your brunch table. Cream ¼ pound (1 stick) softened butter thoroughly with any suggested addition.

Savory Butters:

½ cup grated Cheddar and a pinch of dry mustard

4 tablespoons horseradish

2 tablespoons chopped chutney

½ tablespoon curry powder

¼ cup finely snipped parsley, mint or basil leaves and a few drops of lemon juice

2 tablespoons snipped chives

1 teaspoon chopped fresh tarragon and a few drops of onion juice

2 tablespoons caraway seeds

2 tablespoons sesame seeds

1 tablespoon anchovy paste or 6 mashed anchovy fillets

1 teaspoon Worcestershire sauce

2 skinless, boneless sardines

2 tablespoons well-drained India relish

2 teaspoons lime or lemon juice plus 1 teaspoon grated peel

Sweet Butters:

3 tablespoons honey

2 tablespoons maple sugar

⅓ cup ground walnuts, pecans, cashews, black walnuts or filberts

1 teaspoon vanilla extract plus 1 tablespoon confectioners sugar

1 teaspoon cinnamon plus 1 tablespoon confectioners sugar

½ teaspoon nutmeg plus 2 teaspoons firmly packed light brown sugar

6 ripe strawberries, mashed, plus 1 tablespoon confectioners sugar and a few drops lemon juice

20 ripe raspberries plus 1 tablespoon confectioners sugar and a few drops lemon juice

Eggs are delicate, and they are very sensitive to heat; since they will cook rapidly, they must be cooked at a very low temperature or they will become overcooked and tough. Here are ways to cook eggs so that they will be tender and delicious.

Soft-cooked Eggs: Place in a saucepan the number of eggs you require; cover them with cold water. Place the pan over medium heat and bring the water to the boiling point. Reduce the heat to the point at which the eggs will simmer. Remove the eggs from the water 2 to 3 minutes after simmering begins if the eggs were at room temperature; if eggs came directly from the refrigerator, add 2 minutes to timing.

Medium-cooked Eggs: Time about 4 minutes from the start of simmering —again adding 2 minutes if eggs are cold.

Hard-cooked Eggs: Allow about 15 minutes cooking time after you reduce heat to simmering point. When eggs are done, plunge at once into cold water to prevent further cooking and to keep the yolks from discoloring.

To shell hard-cooked eggs, crack the shell on a hard surface or with a spoon (in either case, be gentle), and then roll each egg between the palms of your hands to loosen the thin, tough membrane just inside the shell. Now the pieces of shell should slide off smoothly. Incidentally, the egg that is difficult to shell is probably too fresh—the fresher the egg, the more trouble you'll have getting the shell off neatly.

To chop hard-cooked eggs, slice (an egg slicer is an inexpensive and very handy kitchen gadget), then mash the eggs with a fork. To slice neatly, if you do not have an egg slicer, use a dampened knife.

Eggs Mollet: These are semisoft-cooked eggs that are kept whole for serving—often used in Eggs in Aspic or in any recipe calling for poached eggs. Bring water to simmering in a saucepan. Lower eggs into water gently; simmer 5 minutes. Run cold water over them until cooled. Break shells gently with back of a spoon and peel, leaving eggs whole.

Coddled Eggs: Lower eggs gently into boiling water. Turn off the heat and cover the pan. Allow 6 minutes for soft-coddled, 8 minutes for firm.

Fried Eggs: Melt in a skillet, over low heat, 1 to 3 tablespoons of butter. Break eggs 1 at a time into a saucer and gently slip them into the skillet—do not crowd. Baste the eggs with the hot butter. Cook over low heat until the eggs are done to your liking. If you want the whites to be firm, cover the skillet as soon as the eggs are in it. If you like the whites soft, add 1 tablespoon hot water, cover the skillet, cook 1 minute, uncover.

Poached Eggs: Unless you poach eggs in individual molds, they are apt to look a bit shaggy. Before serving, trim them neatly with kitchen shears. Butter the bottom of a shallow skillet. Add enough water to cover eggs; salt lightly and add 1 teaspoon white vinegar. Bring water to a boil. Take skillet from heat and break the number of eggs required, 1 at a time, into a saucer and slip each into the water. Let the eggs stand in the hot water 4 to 6 minutes, or until done to your liking. Remove with a skimmer and drain well.

Helpful to know: Eggs may be poached in wine, broth, stock, milk, any of a number of sauces—in fact, in almost any liquid you would like to use.

Scrambled Eggs: Melt in a skillet over low heat 2 tablespoons butter. Break into a bowl the desired number of eggs. Season with salt, pepper and with a tablespoon of cream for each egg. Beat lightly. Pour into skillet. When eggs just begin to set, stir lightly with a fork or a spoon. They may be cooked to any degree of thickness that you like. Eggs will set a bit more, from their own heat, after removal from the skillet—don't overcook.

Shirred (or Baked) Eggs: Butter small casseroles or ramekins, each large enough to accommodate 1 or 2 eggs for 1 serving. Carefully slip eggs into ramekins. Salt lightly and spoon over each egg 1 teaspoon of cream or melted butter. Bake in a preheated 350° oven for 8 to 10 minutes, or until set as you like them. Remember that the eggs will cook a bit, from the heat of the dish, after they are removed from the oven.

Helpful to know: Almost anything cooked and diced, sliced or chopped—meat, vegetables, chicken, for example—may be used as a "bed" on which to bake eggs.

THE LAST-MINUTE BRUNCH

RAID THE PANTRY

Half the fun of a good brunch is its spontaneity. Friends have just dropped by for a cup of coffee—why not make it a brunch? It's a miserably rainy day, so invite friends to sit by the fire and have a cheering drink and a bite to eat. However, to make the last-minute invitation just a little more fun for the hostess, it's nice to know that there is something in the freezer or on the kitchen shelf that will make the brunch a little bit special. Offered here, Smirnoff with a well-flavored juice, a skillet delight made from canned and packaged foods and a dessert that is spectacular.

Smirnoff with Snap-E-Tom
Skillet Delight   Hurry-Up Harlequin Canapés
Quick Corn Relish   Canned Asparagus Marinated in French Dressing
Cheese and Crackers   Hot Refrigerator Rolls
Flaming Pineapple Rumba
Coffee

SMIRNOFF WITH SNAP-E-TOM   1 drink

2 ounces Smirnoff Vodka   **Lime wedge**
  Snap-E-Tom

Place vodka in 8-ounce glass. Add 2 ice cubes and fill with Snap-E-Tom. Cut small slit in lime wedge and hang on edge of glass.

HURRY-UP HARLEQUIN CANAPES   48 canapés

1 package (12 ounces)   3 cans (4 ounces each)
  corn-muffin mix   Vienna sausages
¼ cup grated Parmesan cheese   28 cocktail onions
2 cans (3 ounces each)   ½ cup sliced, sweet pickles
  potted meat   ½ cup sliced, stuffed olives

Prepare corn-muffin mix according to package directions and spread evenly in a well-buttered 15½- x 10½- x 1-inch jelly-roll pan or bake-broil serving tray. Sprinkle top with Parmesan cheese. Spoon potted meat in 3 narrow rows crosswise and at each end of pan. Cut Vienna sausages in half lengthwise; arrange V-shaped rows between rows of potted meat, alternating with the cocktail onions. Arrange rows of sliced pickles and olives in the remaining spaces. Bake in a preheated 400° oven for 20 to 25 minutes, or until browned. Cut into small rectangles.

SKILLET DELIGHT
6 servings

1 cup uncooked rice
½ cup chopped onion
½ cup chopped green pepper
2 tablespoons salad oil
1 can (12 ounces) corned beef, cut in chunks
1 can (4 ounces) Vienna sausages, cut in chunks

2 large tomatoes, peeled, cut in chunks
½ pound mushrooms, sliced
1 can (8½ ounces) peas, drained
½ cup sliced, pitted, ripe olives

In a skillet brown rice, onion and green pepper in oil. Add corned beef, Vienna sausages, tomato chunks, mushrooms and 1½ cups water. Cover and simmer 20 minutes. Stir in peas and olives. Cover and continue to cook 10 minutes, or until rice is done.

QUICK CORN RELISH
4 salad servings

1 can (12 ounces) whole-kernel corn, drained
⅓ cup sweet pickle relish, drained

3 tablespoons mayonnaise
Grey Poupon mustard to taste

Combine all ingredients. Serve as a relish or on lettuce as a salad.

FLAMING PINEAPPLE RUMBA
8 servings

1 can (1 pound, 14 ounces) pineapple slices
Cinnamon
¼ cup butter

1 cup apricot-pineapple preserve
½ cup Don Q Gold Rum
Vanilla ice cream

Drain pineapple. Reserve 6 tablespoons of the syrup. Sprinkle pineapple rings with cinnamon. Melt butter in blazer pan of chafing dish directly over flame. When butter is bubbling hot, add pineapple and sauté until edges are browned. Push to side of pan. Stir in preserve and reserved pineapple syrup. Heat and spoon over pineapple until it looks glazed and transparent. Warm rum gently. Pour over pineapple. Ignite with a wooden match and spoon flaming sauce over pineapple. When flames die down, arrange pineapple slices around scoops of hard ice cream. Spoon hot sauce over the top.

RELAX AND ENJOY

With the help of your freezer, a truly splendid brunch is easy to produce. Most of the hard work has been done long before, and what's left is the fun part. Setting the table, making the drinks, fixing the relishes and putting the frozen food in the oven to heat can all be done with little fuss.

Smirnoff Sours on the Rocks (page 33)
Chicken Puffs   Walnut-Beef Miniatures
Seafood Newburg on Toast Points
or
Chicken Tetrazzini
Crisp Relishes
Frozen Mocha Cake or Rum Duff
Coffee

CHICKEN PUFFS
30 puffs

1 package (8 ounces) refrigerated biscuits
2 egg whites
½ teaspoon salt
½ cup finely minced, cooked chicken
⅓ cup mayonnaise
1 tablespoon minced celery

Carefully pull apart each biscuit to make 3 thin biscuits. Place on unoiled baking sheet and bake in a preheated 400° oven for 6 to 8 minutes, or until golden brown. Remove and cool. Raise oven temperature to 475°. Beat egg whites with salt until stiff peaks form. Carefully fold in remaining ingredients. Drop a heaping teaspoon of mixture on each biscuit. Bake 5 minutes, or until golden brown.
Helpful to know: Puffs may be prepared 1 to 3 hours ahead of time, refrigerated and then baked just before serving.

WALNUT-BEEF MINIATURES
100 meatballs

1 pound ground beef chuck
½ cup soda-cracker crumbs
½ cup finely chopped walnuts
¼ cup canned applesauce
½ teaspoon salt
⅛ teaspoon pepper
⅛ teaspoon nutmeg
2 tablespoons butter
2 tablespoons flour
1½ cups beef bouillon

Combine chuck, cracker crumbs, walnuts and applesauce in a mixing bowl. Add salt, pepper and nutmeg and blend thoroughly. Shape meat lightly into 1-inch cocktail-size balls. Brown meatballs on all sides in melted butter in a large skillet. Remove meatballs as they are browned and set aside. Blend flour into drippings in skillet. Add bouillon and cook, stirring constantly, until mixture thickens slightly and comes to a boil. Taste and add additional salt and pepper if desired. Add meatballs to sauce and simmer 10 to 15 minutes. Cool meatballs as quickly as possible. Ladle into freezer containers, leaving at least 1 inch headroom. Seal, label and freeze.

To serve: Remove from containers and heat in the top of a double boiler over hot water or in a large skillet over very low heat, stirring occasionally. Turn meatballs into a chafing dish and serve piping hot with toothpicks.

SEAFOOD NEWBURG ON TOAST POINTS   8 servings

¼ cup butter	4 eggs yolks, slightly beaten
½ cup flour	½ teaspoon Tabasco sauce
6 cups milk	4 cups cooked seafood—shelled
1½ teaspoons salt	shrimp, lobster *or* crab meat
½ teaspoon paprika	Toast points

Melt butter in a large saucepan. Stir in flour to make a paste. Remove from heat. Stir in milk. Cook, stirring constantly, until mixture thickens and comes to a boil. Add salt and paprika. Stir a small amount of the hot mixture into egg yolks. Return to remaining sauce and stir well. Cook over low heat, stirring constantly, about 3 minutes. Remove from heat and beat in Tabasco. Fold in cooked seafood. Cool pan quickly in a pan of ice water. Spoon mixture into small aluminum containers rather than 1 or 2 large containers, leaving ½ inch headroom. Seal tightly with heavy-duty aluminum foil. Label and freeze.

To serve: Thaw slightly to release from sides of containers. Place in top of a double boiler over boiling water to heat. If desired, just before serving, stir in dry sherry to taste. Serve on toast points.

Helpful to know: Do not keep in freezer longer than 1 month.

CHICKEN TETRAZZINI   5 servings

¼ pound mushrooms, sliced	2 cups diced or slivered
5 tablespoons butter, divided	cooked chicken
5 tablespoons flour	1 package (8 ounces) thin
2 cups chicken broth	spaghetti
1 cup light cream	½ cup grated Parmesan cheese
Salt and pepper to taste	

143

Cook mushrooms in 1 tablespoon of the butter until lightly browned. Set aside. Melt remaining butter in another pan. Stir in flour. Blend in chicken broth. Cook over medium heat, stirring constantly, until smooth and thick. Add cream and season to taste with salt and pepper. Divide sauce in half. Add chicken and mushrooms to one half of the sauce and let stand. Meanwhile cook spaghetti according to package directions, but cook to firm stage. Do not overcook. Drain spaghetti and stir in the other half of the cream sauce. Line a 2-quart casserole with aluminum foil. Allow enough foil to lap over and cover top of casserole. Put spaghetti mixture into casserole. Make a hole in the center of the spaghetti and pour in the cooled chicken mixture. Lap foil over top of spaghetti. Freeze casserole until firm. Remove food-filled foil liner from casserole. Wrap in moisture- and vapor-proof material. Label and seal. Return to freezer.

To serve: Unwrap Tetrazzini and place frozen food in original casserole. Sprinkle Parmesan cheese over top. Cover and bake in a preheated 375° oven for 1 hour and 30 minutes. Remove cover and continue baking 15 minutes, or until mixture is piping hot.

FROZEN MOCHA CAKE
12 servings

Marble pound cake
¼ cup unsweetened cocoa
1 tablespoon instant
   coffee powder
4 eggs

⅛ teaspoon salt
1 cup sugar
1 quart heavy cream
½ cup Arrow Coffee Liqueur

Line sides of a 9-inch springform pan with slices of pound cake, cut about ½ inch thick. Dissolve cocoa and instant coffee powder in ¼ cup boiling water. Cool thoroughly. Beat eggs and salt with an electric mixer until very light and fluffy. Gradually add sugar, beating until thick and lemon-colored. Beat cream until stiff. Fold cocoa mixture, egg mixture and liqueur into cream. Blend lightly but thoroughly. Pour into cake-lined pan. Overwrap with moisture- and vapor-proof material. Seal, label and freeze.

To serve: Remove cake from freezer. Remove wrappings and loosen sides from springform pan. Remove pan rim. Place cake on a serving plate. Garnish with whipped cream and shaved chocolate if desired.

RUM DUFF
6 to 8 servings

2 cups canned applesauce
¼ cup sugar
3 tablespoons Don Q White Rum

1 tablespoon grated orange peel
2 cups gingersnap crumbs
½ cup heavy cream

Combine applesauce, sugar, rum, orange peel and gingersnaps. Stir until well mixed. Chill. Whip cream and fold into applesauce mixture. Pile into sherbet glasses and serve.

EGGS, BREADS AND YOU

Any Sunday or any holiday, for any occasion, fresh homemade breads from your freezer will be the star of a quick and easy brunch. While the breads are defrosting and the welcome drink is being passed, whip up a batch of scrambled eggs to complete a brunch fit for a king.

Smirnoff White Fizzes
Mushroomed Scrambled Eggs
Eggs Delmonico
Banana Loaf   Gugelhupf
Peanut Honey Buns
Butter   Fresh Strawberry Jam
Coffee

SMIRNOFF WHITE FIZZ
1 drink

2 ounces Smirnoff Vodka
Juice of ½ lemon
1 egg white
1 teaspoon confectioners sugar

1 tablespoon light cream
½ teaspoon orange flower water
Carbonated water

Combine all ingredients except carbonated water and shake well with cracked ice. Strain into 12-ounce glass. Fill with carbonated water. Stir.

MUSHROOMED SCRAMBLED EGGS
12 servings

1 can (10½ ounces) condensed cream
of mushroom soup, undiluted
2 dozens eggs
1 pint dairy sour cream

1 teaspoon salt
¼ teaspoon pepper
¼ cup butter

Heat mushroom soup until piping hot and pour into a chafing dish over hot water. Break eggs into a large mixing bowl. Add sour cream, salt and pepper and beat with a rotary beater until well blended. Melt butter in a large skillet and pour in egg mixture. Stir slowly from bottom. Cook until eggs are just set. Do not overcook. Spoon eggs into mushroom soup and serve. *Helpful to know:* The mushroom soup will keep the eggs moist and hot.

EGGS DELMONICO
6 servings

¼ cup butter
1 tablespoon minced onion
¼ cup flour
2 cups light cream
½ cup grated Cheddar cheese
1 tablespoon finely snipped
parsley

1 teaspoon salt
¼ teaspoon pepper
1 cup sautéed, sliced mushrooms
3 slices boiled ham,
cut in slivers
6 hard-cooked eggs (page 137),
shelled and sliced

Melt butter in a saucepan. Add onion and cook until tender but not browned. Stir in flour. Remove from heat and stir in cream. Cook over medium heat, stirring constantly, until smooth and thickened. Add cheese, parsley, salt and pepper and stir until blended. Mix in mushrooms and ham. Carefully fold in eggs. Keep warm in a chafing dish.

BANANA LOAF
1 loaf

½ cup butter, softened
½ cup sugar
2 eggs
1½ cups mashed bananas
½ cup chopped walnuts

2 cups sifted flour
½ teaspoon baking powder
½ teaspoon baking soda
½ teaspoon salt

Cream together butter and sugar until light and fluffy. Beat in eggs. Blend in bananas and nuts. Sift together flour, baking powder, baking soda and salt. Add to creamed mixture and beat only until blended. Turn into an oiled loaf pan 9 x 5 x 3 inches. Bake in a preheated 350° oven for 45 to 50 minutes. Cool in pan on a wire rack for 10 minutes. Turn out of pan onto a rack to finish cooling. Wrap loaf in moisture- and vapor-proof material. Seal, label and freeze.
To serve: Let stand at room temperature until thawed.

GUGELHUPF
1 loaf

½ cup milk
½ cup sugar
½ teaspoon salt
¼ cup butter
1 package or cake yeast, active dry or compressed
2 eggs, beaten

2 cups flour
2 tablespoons fine, dry bread crumbs
14 to 16 whole blanched almonds
½ cup seedless raisins
½ teaspoon grated lemon peel

Scald milk; stir in sugar, salt and butter. Cool to lukewarm. Measure ¼ cup warm (105°-115°) water into a large warm bowl. Sprinkle or crumble in yeast; stir until dissolved. Stir in lukewarm milk mixture. Add beaten eggs and flour. Beat vigorously about 5 minutes. Cover; let rise in a warm place, free from draft, until doubled in bulk, about 1½ hours. Butter a 1½-quart casserole or gugelhupf mold. Sprinkle with dry bread crumbs. Arrange almonds on bottom of pan. Stir batter down. Beat thoroughly. Stir in raisins and lemon peel. Carefully spoon batter into mold. Let rise in a warm place, free from draft, until doubled in bulk, about 1 hour. Bake in a preheated 350° oven for 50 minutes. Turn bread out of pan onto wire rack and cool thoroughly. Wrap in moisture- and vapor-proof material. Seal, label and freeze.
To serve: Let stand at room temperature until thawed.

PEANUT HONEY BUNS

2 dozens

½ cup milk
¼ cup butter
¼ cup sugar
½ teaspoon salt
2 packages or cakes yeast,
  active dry or compressed
1 egg
3¼ cups (about) flour
½ cup chopped salted peanuts

⅓ cup dark brown sugar,
  firmly packed
⅔ cup honey
4 tablespoons melted
  butter, divided
½ cup chopped salted peanuts
½ cup dark brown sugar,
  firmly packed

Scald milk. Stir in butter, sugar and salt. Cool to lukewarm. Measure ½ cup warm (105°-115°) water into a large warm bowl. Sprinkle or crumble in yeast; stir until dissolved. Add lukewarm milk mixture, egg and 2 cups of the flour. Beat until smooth. Stir in enough additional flour to make a soft dough. Turn out on a lightly floured board. Knead about 10 minutes until smooth and elastic. Place in an oiled bowl, turning once to oil top of dough. Cover and let rise in a warm place, free from draft, until doubled in bulk, about 40 minutes. Combine ½ cup of the chopped peanuts, ⅓ cup dark brown sugar, honey and 3 tablespoons melted butter. Mix until blended. Divide this mixture evenly among 24 oiled muffin cups, 2¾ x 1½ inches. When dough is doubled in bulk, punch down. Turn out onto a lightly floured board and divide in half. Roll out half into a rectangle 12 x 9 inches. Brush lightly with remaining melted butter. Combine remaining ½ cup peanuts with ½ cup brown sugar. Sprinkle rectangle with half of this mixture. Roll tightly from 12-inch side, jelly-roll fashion. Seal edges firmly. Cut into 1-inch slices. Place, cut side up, into 12 of the prepared muffin cups. Repeat with remaining half of dough and peanut—brown-sugar mixture. Cover pans. Let rise in a warm place, free from draft, for about 40 minutes, or until doubled in bulk. Bake in a preheated 375° oven for 15 to 20 minutes. Turn out of pans immediately onto wire racks. When cool, put buns on a baking sheet, place in freezer and freeze until firm. Remove from freezer and package in moisture- and vapor-proof material. Seal, label and freeze.

To serve: Remove buns from freezer and remove wrappings. Let stand at room temperature until thawed or place on a baking sheet and heat in a preheated 300° oven for about 10 minutes.

FRESH STRAWBERRY JAM

2 cups

1 quart fully ripe strawberries
4 cups sugar

1 box fruit pectin

Wash glasses and lids or plastic containers, scald and drain. Wash and hull berries. Completely crush berries, one layer at a time. Measure 2 cups of the crushed fruit into a large bowl. Add sugar and stir thoroughly. Combine pectin and ¾ cup water in a small pan. Bring to a boil and boil for *1 minute,* stirring constantly. Stir immediately into strawberries. Continue stirring for 3 minutes. A few sugar crystals will remain. Quickly ladle into glasses. Cover at once with tight lids. Let stand at room temperature until set; this may take up to 24 hours. Store jam in the freezer. It may be kept in refrigerator if the jam is to be used within 3 weeks.

HAVE SOME FUN

For this brunch all has been done the day before and stashed away in the refrigerator. Put out the pâté with a choice of rye-bread rounds or crackers, and cut the bologna in wedges for people to nibble while the puff is baking. The brown-and-serve sausages cook themselves. Sprinkle canned peach halves with a little brown sugar or maple syrup and pop under the broiler for just a couple of minutes, long enough to heat through. With warm cake and buns and plenty of hot coffee, you are all set to have a good time yourself.

Smirnoff Screwdrivers (page 17)
Vermouth Liver Pâté with Crackers   Ribbon Bologna Wedges
Egg-and-Cheese Puff
Brown-and-Serve Sausages   Broiled Peach Halves
Quick Pecan Ring   Quick Caramel Buns
Orange-Honey Cubes
Coffee

VERMOUTH LIVER PATE   2 cups

1 **pound chicken livers**
1 **teaspoon garlic sa**
½ **teaspoon powdered rosemary**
½ **teaspoon paprika**

1 **tablespoon flour**
¼ **cup butter**
¾ **cup dry vermouth**

Rinse and drain chicken livers. Pat dry with paper towels. Dredge with seasonings mixed with flour. Melt butter in a skillet. Add chicken livers and cook to a rich golden brown. Add ½ cup of the vermouth; cover and simmer until livers are tender. Remove from heat; add remaining vermouth and cool. Blend mixture in an electric blender until smooth. Turn into a bowl. Cover and refrigerate several hours or overnight.

149

RIBBON BOLOGNA WEDGES

1 jar (5 ounces) cheese spread
with olives and pimiento

12 thin slices large
bologna sausage

¼ cup finely chopped
walnuts *or* pecans

Finely snipped parsley

Spread cheese evenly on bologna slices. Sprinkle each slice with nuts. Pile 6 slices on top of each other. Sprinkle parsley on top. Cover with plastic wrap and chill. To serve, cut each pile into 16 wedges and insert a colored toothpick in each.

EGG-AND-CHEESE PUFF

8 servings

16 slices white bread
Butter

½ pound Cheddar cheese, grated

1 medium-size onion, thinly
sliced

6 eggs, well beaten

1 quart milk

1 teaspoon salt

¼ teaspoon white pepper

Trim crust from bread and butter each slice. Arrange 8 slices, buttered side down, in the bottom of a well-oiled rectangular baking dish, about 9 x 13½ inches. Cover with cheese and onion. Top with remaining slices of bread, buttered side up. Combine eggs, milk, salt and pepper. Pour over bread. Cover pan with aluminum foil and refrigerate overnight. Remove foil and place in a pan of hot water. Bake in a preheated 350° oven for 1 hour, or until puffed and lightly browned on top. Serve immediately.

QUICK PECAN RING

8 to 10 servings

2 packages (8 ounces each)
refrigerated butterflake rolls

⅔ cup sugar

½ teaspoon cinnamon

½ cup milk

¼ cup chopped pecans

½ cup confectioners sugar

1 tablespoon milk

¼ teaspoon vanilla extract

Chopped pecans

Separate refrigerated dough into 24 rolls. Combine sugar and cinnamon. Dip each roll in the milk and then in cinnamon-sugar mixture, turning to coat all sides. Place half the rolls, slightly overlapping, in bottom of an oiled 6½-cup ring mold. Sprinkle with chopped pecans. Add remaining rolls, forming a second layer of overlapping rolls. Bake in a preheated 375° oven for 25 to 30 minutes, or until golden brown. Turn onto serving plate immediately. Combine confectioners sugar and milk and blend well. Stir in vanilla. Drizzle over top and sides of ring. Sprinkle with additional chopped pecans.

QUICK CARAMEL BUNS

10 buns

½ cup light brown sugar,
firmly packed

⅓ cup butter, melted

1 tablespoon light corn syrup

½ cup coarsely chopped walnuts

1 package (9½ ounces) refrigerated
flaky biscuits

In a small mixing bowl blend sugar, butter, syrup and walnuts. Spoon a heaping tablespoon of the mixture into each of ten 3-inch muffin-pan cups. Open biscuits according to package directions. Place 1 biscuit in each cup on top of mixture. Bake in a preheated 375° oven for 12 to 14 minutes, or until tops are golden brown. Remove from oven and immediately invert muffin pan onto a large piece of aluminum foil. Let pan remain over buns for 1 minute. Gently remove pan.

ORANGE-HONEY CUBES
6 servings

1 loaf unsliced day-old white bread
¼ cup light brown sugar, firmly packed
¾ teaspoon cinnamon

2 tablespoons frozen orange juice concentrate, undiluted
2 tablespoons honey
¼ cup melted butter
¼ cup coarsely chopped nuts

Cut crust from top and sides of bread. Cut lengthwise through center of loaf, almost through to bottom crust. Then cut crosswise to form 8 cubes. Combine sugar, cinnamon, orange juice, honey, butter and nuts. Stir until well blended. Pour mixture over bread, letting some run down into cuts and over top. Tie bread loosely around sides with a string. Place on a baking sheet. Bake in a preheated 350° oven for 10 to 15 minutes.

BRUNCH IT YOURSELF

Here are more good-for-brunch dishes—around which you can build your own, suit-yourself brunch menus.

SMIRNOFF TWISTER
1 drink

1½ ounces Smirnoff Vodka
Juice and peel of ⅓ lime

Seven-Up

Put 3 ice cubes into an 8-ounce highball glass. Add the vodka and lime juice and peel. Fill glass with Seven-Up and stir gently.

SMIRNOFF PURPLE SNAPPER
1 drink

1½ ounces Smirnoff Vodka

Grape juice, chilled

Place 2 ice cubes and vodka in a tall highball glass. Fill glass with chilled grape juice.

SMIRNOFF SALT LICK
1 drink

Lemon juice
Fine salt
2 ounces Smirnoff Vodka

2 ounces grapefruit juice, chilled
2 ounces tonic, chilled

Moisten rim of an 8-ounce glass with lemon juice; then swirl in fine salt to form a frosted ring around edge. Put an ice cube into the glass. Add vodka, grapefruit juice and tonic. Stir lightly.

GOUGERE

½ cup butter
1 cup sifted flour
½ teaspoon salt

4 eggs
1 cup grated Swiss cheese

Bring 1 cup boiling water and butter to a boil in a medium-size saucepan. When the butter is melted, add the flour and salt all at once. Reduce the heat and stir vigorously until the mixture leaves the sides of the pan and begins to gather into a ball. Remove from heat and add the eggs, 1 at a time, beating vigorously after each addition. Continue beating until the mixture has a satin sheen. Stir in the cheese. Drop by teaspoonfuls onto a baking sheet. Bake in a preheated 400° oven for 20 minutes. Cool thoroughly. Place on a baking sheet and freeze until firm. Wrap in moisture- and vapor-proof material. Seal, label and freeze.

To serve: Remove puffs from container and place on a baking sheet. Let stand for 10 minutes. Heat in a 350° oven for 10 minutes. Serve hot.

BATONNETS DE FROMAGE

50 bâtonnets

3 tablespoons butter
5 tablespoons flour
1½ cups milk
¾ teaspoon salt
¾ cup grated Parmesan cheese

2 egg yolks, beaten
Flour
1 egg, beaten
¼ cup milk
Fine, dry bread crumbs

Melt butter in saucepan. Add flour; stir well. Slowly mix in 1½ cups milk, salt. Cook over medium heat, stirring constantly, until mixture thickens and comes to a boil. Add cheese and stir until cheese is melted. Add a little of the hot mixture to the beaten egg yolks, mix well and return egg mixture to saucepan. Stir well. Cook over very low heat, stirring constantly, 3 to 4 minutes longer. Line a 5- x 9-inch pan with aluminum foil and pour in mixture. Mixture should be about ¾ inch deep. Chill overnight. When firm and cold, turn out onto a lightly floured board. Peel off foil and cut into little rectangles, ½ x 1 inch. Roll in flour, then dip in a mixture of 1 egg beaten with ¼ cup milk. Roll in bread crumbs. Place on a baking sheet and freeze. When firm, package in small foil pans. Wrap in moisture- and vapor-proof material. Seal, label and freeze. These will keep well for about 6 weeks.

To serve: Remove desired number from freezer. Fry a few at a time in deep oil heated to 375°. Drain on paper towels. Serve piping hot.

CHICKEN-NUT PUFFS

100 puffs

1 cup chicken broth
½ cup salad oil
2 teaspoons seasoned salt
1 teaspoon celery seed
1 tablespoon dried parsley flakes
2 teaspoons Worcestershire sauce

1 cup sifted flour
4 eggs
¾ cup finely minced,
  cooked chicken
⅓ cup chopped, toasted,
  blanched almonds

In a saucepan combine chicken broth, salad oil, salt, celery seed, parsley flakes and Worcestershire sauce. Bring to a boil. Add the flour all at once and stir rapidly over low heat until mixture leaves the sides of the pan and forms a smooth, compact ball. Remove from heat. Add eggs, 1 at a time, beating very hard with a spoon until mixture is smooth and shiny. Add chicken and almonds and blend well. Drop by half spoonfuls onto a lightly oiled baking sheet. Bake in a preheated 450° oven for 10 to 15 minutes, or until puffed and lightly browned. Cool quickly. Place on a baking sheet and freeze until firm. Place puffs in moisture- and vapor-proof material. Seal, label and freeze.

To serve: Place frozen puffs on a baking sheet. Heat in a preheated 250° oven for 10 to 15 minutes. Serve hot.

HAM 'N' CHEESE BALLS   40 appetizers

½ cup butter

1½ cups shredded Cheddar cheese

¼ cup finely chopped baked ham

¼ teaspoon Worcestershire sauce

Dash of cayenne

1 cup sifted flour

In a mixing bowl combine butter, cheese, ham and seasonings. Blend in flour and mix well. Shape dough into balls the size of large marbles and place on baking sheet. Bake in a preheated 350° oven for 15 to 18 minutes. Serve piping hot or spread uncooked balls out in a single layer in a shallow pan. Place in a freezer and freeze until hard. Remove from freezer and pack in freezer bags.

To serve: Remove the number desired for serving and bake as above.

WILD-RICE—CHICKEN SUPREME   6 to 8 servings

1 box (6 ounces) long-grain and wild rice

¼ cup butter

⅓ cup chopped onion

⅓ cup flour

1 teaspoon salt

Pinch of pepper

½ cup milk

½ cup light cream

1 cup chicken broth

2 cups cooked, cubed chicken

⅓ cup chopped pimiento

⅓ cup snipped parsley

3 tablespoons chopped, blanched almonds

Cook rice according to package directions. Melt butter in a saucepan. Cook onion in hot butter until light golden. Add flour, salt and pepper. Remove from heat and stir in milk, cream and chicken broth. Cook, stirring constantly, until smooth and thickened. Combine rice, chicken, sauce, pimiento and parsley. Mix well. Pour into an oiled casserole. Sprinkle almonds over top. Bake in a preheated 400° oven for 30 minutes, or until piping hot. Or turn unbaked mixture into a foil-lined casserole. Cool and freeze. Remove from casserole. Wrap with moisture- and vapor-proof material and return to freezer.

To serve: Remove freezer wrappings. Return foil-wrapped food to casserole and bake in a preheated 375° oven for about 1 hour, or until bubbly.

CHICKEN IN WHITE WINE

4 to 6 servings

3 whole chicken breasts, split
¼ cup butter
½ cup finely chopped onion
¼ pound mushrooms, sliced
1 clove garlic, crushed
2 tablespoons flour

Dash of salt
Dash of pepper
Pinch of thyme
2 chicken-bouillon cubes
½ cup dry white wine

Remove skin from chicken pieces. Heat butter in a dutch oven. Brown chicken pieces lightly in dutch oven, 2 at a time. Remove chicken pieces. Add onion, mushrooms and garlic to butter in dutch oven. Cook, stirring, a few minutes. Remove from heat and stir in flour and seasonings. Gradually stir in 1½ cups water. Crumble in bouillon cubes. Cook over moderate heat, stirring constantly, until mixture is smooth and thickened. Add white wine. Add chicken pieces and simmer 10 minutes. Cool quickly by immersing dutch oven in ice water. Line a shallow 1½-quart casserole with aluminum foil. Pour chicken mixture into casserole. Freeze until solid. Remove foil-wrapped chicken and wrap in moisture- and vapor-proof material. Seal, label and freeze.

To serve: Remove wrapping from chicken and return to casserole. Cover and bake in a preheated 400° oven for 45 minutes, stirring lightly once in a while. Remove cover and bake 15 to 20 minutes, or until tender.

SHERRIED CHICKEN

4 to 6 servings

4 chicken breasts, split,
  boned and skinned
1½ teaspoons salt
¼ teaspoon pepper
1 teaspoon paprika
¾ cup butter, divided

½ pound mushrooms, sliced
¼ cup flour
1⅓ cups chicken consommé
6 tablespoons dry sherry
1 can (15 ounces) artichoke
  hearts

Sprinkle chicken pieces with a mixture of salt, pepper and paprika. Melt 4 tablespoons of the butter in a skillet and cook chicken pieces until lightly browned on all sides. Line a shallow 2-quart casserole with aluminum foil. Place chicken pieces in casserole. Place remaining butter in the skillet; add mushrooms and cook gently a few minutes. Add flour and stir until blended. Slowly stir in chicken consommé. Cook over medium heat, stirring constantly, until mixture is smooth and slightly thickened. Stir in sherry. Cool sauce quickly by immersing skillet in ice water. Drain artichoke hearts and arrange over chicken. Pour cooled sauce over top of chicken. Place casserole in freezer and freeze until firm. Remove foil-lined food from casserole and wrap in moisture- and vapor-proof material. Seal, label and return to freezer.

To serve: Remove wrapping from food and return to original casserole. Cover casserole and bake in a preheated 350° oven for 1 hour. Remove cover, turn up heat to 375° and continue baking for 15 to 30 minutes, or until chicken is tender and piping hot.

PARTY BEEF

8 to 10 servings

3 tablespoons salad oil
2 garlic cloves, minced
3 pounds beef chuck, cut
   into 2-inch cubes
2 cans (8 ounces each)
   tomato sauce
2 cups dry red wine
¾ teaspoon basil

½ teaspoon thyme
2 teaspoons salt
¼ teaspoon pepper
16 small white onions, peeled
8 carrots, scraped and sliced
   diagonally
2 packages (10 ounces each)
   frozen peas

Heat oil in a heavy dutch oven. Add garlic and beef and cook over medium heat until meat is browned. Add tomato sauce, wine, 1 cup water and seasonings. Cover and simmer over low heat for 1 hour. Add onions and carrots and continue cooking 30 minutes. Cool quickly by immersing dutch oven in ice water. Turn mixture into freezer containers, leaving at least ½-inch headroom on the top. Seal, label and freeze.

To serve: Run hot water on outsides of containers to loosen food. Place blocks of food in heavy dutch oven. Cook over very low heat, stirring occasionally, until food has thawed. Add frozen peas, bring up heat to moderate and simmer until peas are cooked and meat is tender.

TAMALE PIE

8 servings

2 onions, thinly sliced
5 tablespoons salad oil
3 cloves garlic, minced
1½ pounds beef chuck, cut into
   ½-inch cubes
1½ teaspoons salt
2 tablespoons chili powder
1 can (1 pound, 13 ounces)
   tomatoes
1½ cups sliced, pitted,
   ripe olives

1 can (12 ounces) whole-
   kernel corn
½ cup chopped green pepper
2 teaspoons salt
1½ teaspoons chili powder
1½ cups yellow cornmeal
½ cup grated American cheese
   Paprika

Brown onions lightly in hot salad oil. Remove onions. Add garlic and beef cubes. Brown lightly. Add 1½ teaspoons salt, 2 tablespoons chili powder, tomatoes, olives, corn, green pepper and browned onions. Cover and simmer slowly about 1½ hours. Cool mixture. Add 2 teaspoons salt and 1½ teaspoons chili powder to 4½ cups boiling water. Slowly add cornmeal, stirring constantly. Cook over low heat 15 minutes, stirring occasionally. Line an oiled baking dish, 9 inches in diameter, with a layer of this cornmeal mush. Pour meat mixture carefully over the cornmeal. Cover with remaining mush. Wrap pan in moisture- and vapor-proof material. Seal, label and freeze.

To serve: Unwrap pan. Cover and bake in a preheated 375° oven for 1 hour and 30 minutes. Top with grated cheese and sprinkle with paprika. Continue baking 15 minutes longer, or until piping hot.

QUICK APPLE CRISP

6 servings

2 cans (1 pound each)
pie-sliced apples
1 package (6 ounces)
butterscotch-flavored morsels
2 tablespoons
quick-cooking tapioca

1 tablespoon lemon juice
½ cup flour
½ cup sugar
1 teaspoon cinnamon
½ cup firm butter

Combine apples, butterscotch morsels and tapioca in a 1½-quart casserole. Sprinkle with lemon juice. Combine flour, sugar and cinnamon in a small bowl. Cut in butter with a pastry blender or two knives until mixture resembles cornmeal. Sprinkle over apple mixture. Bake in a preheated 375° oven for 40 minutes. Serve warm with cream or ice cream, if desired.

APPLE PIE

6 servings

Pastry for a 2-crust pie
1 teaspoon flour
1 tablespoon sugar
5 to 6 cooking apples, peeled,
cored and thinly sliced

¾ cup sugar
1 teaspoon cinnamon
¼ teaspoon salt
2 tablespoons butter

Roll out half the pastry on a lightly floured board in a circle large enough to fit a 9-inch pie plate. Fit pastry into pie plate. Combine the flour with 1 tablespoon sugar. Sprinkle in bottom of shell. Place apples in shell. Mix ¾ cup sugar, cinnamon and salt and sprinkle over apples. Dot with butter. Roll out remaining pastry and place on top of apples. Seal and flute the edges. Place pie in freezer and freeze until firm. Wrap in moisture- and vapor-proof material. Seal, label and return to freezer.
To serve: Unwrap frozen pie. Cut slits in top crust. Bake in a preheated 400° oven for 1 hour and 15 minutes, or until apples are tender and crust is golden brown.

FROZEN STRAWBERRY PIE

8 servings

1½ cups vanilla wafer crumbs
½ cup finely chopped nuts
½ cup butter, melted
1½ cups sliced fresh strawberries

1 cup sugar
1 egg white
1 cup dairy sour cream

Combine crumbs, nuts and butter in a small bowl. Blend thoroughly. Press firmly on bottom and sides of a 10-inch pie pan. Bake in a preheated 350° oven for 8 to 10 minutes. Cool. Combine strawberries, sugar and egg white in the large bowl of an electric mixer Beat at medium-high speed until soft peaks form, about 10 minutes. Gently fold in sour cream. Mound into crust and place in freezer. Freeze until firm. Remove and wrap in moisture- and vapor-proof material. Seal, label and freeze.
To serve: Remove from freezer and let stand unwrapped at room temperature until almost thawed. Remove wrapping and serve.

INDEX

Smirnoff and Cherry, 37
Smirnoff and Guinness, 78
Smirnoff and Port, 70
Smirnoff and Tonic, 66
Smirnoff Apple Dandy, 132
Smirnoff Bloody Bullshot, 27
Smirnoff Bloody Mary, 9
Smirnoff Burnished Brass, 70
Smirnoff Cape Codder, 14
Smirnoff Cup, 130
Smirnoff Curaçao Screwdriver, 70
Smirnoff Dill Mary, 70
Smirnoff Election Punch, 126
Smirnoff Festive Punch, 42
Smirnoff Fruity Punch, 50
Smirnoff Gibson, 101
Smirnoff Grape Froth, 53
Smirnoff Grasshopper, 21
Smirnoff Hawkshot, 63
Smirnoff Huntsman, 101
Smirnoff Lime Dry, 84
Smirnoff Margaretta, 103
Smirnoff Martini, 76
Smirnoff Martini on the Rocks, 11
Smirnoff Midwinter Punch, 52
Smirnoff Milk Punch, 30
Smirnoff Mint Sparkle, 123
Smirnoff Mule, 120
Smirnoff 'n' Cider, 107
Smirnoff Orange-Cider Punch, 52
Smirnoff Plum Punch, 39
Smirnoff Purple Snapper, 151
Smirnoff Quencher, 101
Smirnoff Raspberry Cooler, 52
Smirnoff Royal Ade, 21
Smirnoff Salt Lick, 151
Smirnoff Salty Dog, 28
Smirnoff Sangaree, 59
Smirnoff Screwdriver, 17
Smirnoff Smash, 18
Smirnoff Sour, 33
Smirnoff Special, 132
Smirnoff Spiced Punch, 52
Smirnoff Splendid, 120
Smirnoff Storm, 92
Smirnoff Stormcloud, 21
Smirnoff Strawberry Flip, 52
Smirnoff Summer Martini, 37
Smirnoff Twister, 151
Smirnoff White Fizz, 146
Smirnoff White Russian, 27
Smirnoff with Snap-E-Tom, 139
Smirnoff Yellow Fever, 35

BREADS AND OTHER BAKED TREATS
Banana Loaf, 147
Best-Ever Biscuits, 31
Cheddar Bread Sticks, 94
Cheese Biscuits, 134
Cheese-filled Blintzes, 18
Cheese Pizza, 90
Cinnamon Coffee Braid, 96
Corn-Bread Squares, 64

Corn Dollars, 71
Corn Fritters, 23
Cornmeal Pancakes, 50
Cottage Spoon Bread, 55
Crepes, 40
Crepes Ratatouille, 41
Hospitality Wafers, 11
Hot Cross Buns, 49
Kulich, 47
Lobster Crepes, 40
Molletes de Calabaza
    (Pumpkin Muffins), 106
Mushroom-and-Cheese Pizza, 91
Orange-Honey Cubes, 151
Orange Waffles with Butterscotch
    Sauce, 72
Pancake Puffs, 15
Peanut Honey Buns, 148
Pecan Buttermilk Muffins, 35
Pepperoni Pizza, 90
Pizza Crust, 90
Popovers, 34
Potato Waffles, 50
Quick Caramel Buns, 150
Quick Crescents, 10
Quick Pecan Ring, 150
Snails, 17
Sour-Cream Biscuits, 47
Spicy Honey Bread, 62

CAKES AND COOKIES
Almond Slices, 76
Angel Food Cake, 25
Black-Walnut Crisps, 84
Breakfast Cake, 19
Butter Cookies, 41
Cheesecake Melba, 94
Chocolate Coffee Roll, 24
Cream Twists, 29
Dundee Cake, 75
Filling for Chocolate Coffee Roll, 25
Florentines, 86
Fluffy Cream-Cheese Icing, 44
Frozen Mocha Cake, 145
Gugelhupf, 147
Kourambiedes (Greek Clove Cookies), 116
Lemon Wonder Cake, 57
Lucia Wonder Cake, 57
Madeleines, 68
Mahogany Cake, 64
Mocha Frosting, 66
Mocha Wonder Cake, 58
Orange Baba, 13
Orange-Plus Wonder Cake, 58
Pecan Log, 25
Shortnin' Bread, 111
Sugar-and-Spice Wonder Cake, 58
Swedish Apple Cake, 100
Torta Ricotta (Cheese Layer Cake), 119
Virginia Wonder Cake, 58
Walnut Devil's Food Birthday Cake, 44
White Fruitcake, 26
Wine-Walnut Wonder Cake, 58